SHOPIFY

EMPIRE

Dominate Search Results, Sell More, and Change Your World

Josh Highland Giese

Special thanks to Amy Highland, Jason Keller, Curtis Rissi, Luis Majano, Ryan Youngman, Nikk Figurin, Ramchand Rao, Kalen Gibbons, Eric Gregson, Tommy Green, Jeff Bacher, ICW, CXCB, and Tim Ferriss.

Extra special thanks go to Rhian Beutler.
Thank you for your dedication to this project.

You will search for me,
and when you search for me with all your heart,
you will find me.

-- Jeremiah 29:13

Table of Contents

ACKNOWLEDGMENTS   ix

ABOUT THE AUTHOR   x

Introduction   1

1. Understanding SEO   5
   Why SEO Matters   5
   Algorithms - Ingredients and Recipes   8
   Moving Targets   9
   Expectations   10

2. Building The Foundation   13
   Domain Names   14
   Themes   18

3. Structured For Success   23
   Structure – search engines and customers LOVE it!   23
   The Structural Elements of a Shopify Store   24
   Executing the plan   29
   Navigation   30
   Remove the Barriers   32
   The Fundamentals Are Foundational   33

4. Types Of SEO   35
   Optimization vs. Marketing   36

5. On-Site Optimization   37
   Content is King   37
   Understanding Meta Tags and Meta Data   39
   Title, Description, Keywords - The Meta Data Trinity   39
   The Title Tag   39
   The Description Meta Tag   43
   The Keyword Meta Tag   46

Tuning your products 47

Things to avoid 48

(Do not) Use Duplicate Content 49

6. Image Optimization 51

SEO For Your Product Images 51

7. Backlinks 57

Backlinks 57

8. The Social Factors 73

Social Gravity 74

Getting Your Content Shared 75

Engagement 78

Measure, Evaluate, Adjust 79

9. A Deeper Dive Into SEO Strategies 83

Code Tuning 83

Reducing Bounce Rates 87

Dealing With Out Of Stock Products 89

10. SEO Tools 95

Shopify Grader 95

Shopify Reports 97

Google Analytics 101

Google Webmaster Tools 107

Bing Webmaster Tools 117

Google Alerts 122

11. Apps For SEO 125

SEO Report Apps for Shopify 125

Product Reviews 126

12. Competition Research 131

Search Engine Result Page (SERP) Analysis 131

On-Site Content Analysis 132

On-Site Tech Analysis 132

Backlink Analysis 132

Engagement Analysis 132

Competitive Analysis Tools 132

Helpful Competition Analysis Tools 133

13. A Drop In Rankings – What To Do 135

Possible Reasons For A Dip In Search Rankings 135

An Increase In Competition 135

Major Changes To Your Site 136

Google Changed The Rules Again 136

Search Engine Penalties 137

14. No Shortcuts To Success 139

Term Glossary 141

ACKNOWLEDGMENTS

To my wife Amy for always being there, and my sons Jackson and Abraham for inspiring me without saying a single word.

10% of all proceeds from this book will be donated to The Pratyasha Foundation. A non-profit organization dedicated to the inspiration, nourishment, education, and the support of children in India.

http://ThePratyashaFoundation.org

ABOUT THE AUTHOR

Josh Highland Giese
Better known as Josh Highland, owns and operates NewLeaf Labs, a software and services company focused on the Shopify platform. NewLeaf Labs has been a certified Shopify Expert since 2011 and has assisted hundreds of Shopify shop owners.

Josh holds a degree in Computer Science from the University of California Riverside (UCR), and currently resides in Redlands, California with his wife Amy and son Jackson.

Twitter: @JoshHighland
Email: JoshHighland@NewLeafLabs.com

RANDOM FACTS ABOUT JOSH:

- Wrote his first computer program on a TI-99/4A at age 7
- Created a social network in 2001 - notPopular.com
- Developed and released 10 iPhone / iPad apps.
- Has taught a college course on iPhone development.
- Can solve a Rubik's cube in less than one minute.

INTRODUCTION

I have been addicted to technology my entire life. In 1986, at the age of seven, I wrote my first computer program on a TI-99/4A, and in the early 90's I got my first dial up modem. Back then, the Internet was young and full of promise. I saw its potential and started to learn how the Internet worked. I launched my first website in late 1993. At the time websites were discovered through trade magazines, email lists, and online directories. The "Information Super Highway," as it was called, was a simple place. Search engines, as we know them today, did not really exist.

My interest in computers and the Internet led me to pursue a degree in computer science. In 1998, while working in one of the University of California Riverside computer labs, one of the graduate students showed me a website that some people from Stanford had recently launched. He swore that it was going to change the Internet once it caught on. The site was Google.com.

I remember thinking that Google's interface was extremely simplistic, even for the time. The first thing I searched for was my own name. The search results that were returned included my personal website. Instantly Google had better search results than the major search engines of the time. It amazed me how a startup company with servers sitting in a garage could have better results than Yahoo. Yahoo was HUGE!

I had to find out how Google got their results, and how they were sorted and ranked. I was not the only one interested in this information. An entire industry based around "Search Engine Optimization", or SEO, was born as Google quickly took over the Internet.

As people learned to manipulate search results, Google began adapting their methods and formulas for calculating ranks. This created the digital arms race between the SEO industry and Google that still exists today. Due to the nature of SEO, the industry is always evolving. Despite the changes, there have remained several SEO practices and techniques that search engines consistently value. These constants are the areas that I focus on when creating a SEO strategy for a client.

In 2008 I read *"The Four Hour Work Week"* by Tim Ferriss and decided to create a product to sell online. I needed an easy-to-use ecommerce solution to sell my products. I discovered Shopify.com and fell in love with it. I was instantly impressed, and recommended Shopify to several of my clients. They quickly moved their online stores to the Shopify platform. As I became more involved with the Shopify, I discovered that their support for SEO lacked some advanced features. Like any good programmer would do, I solved the problem by writing software to fill the gaps I had found.

I developed an app that helps manage meta tags and other SEO related information. I installed the app on several of my client's stores, and the results were astounding. In 2011, one my clients became one of the top grossing stores on the Shopify platform.

Due to the success I witnessed, I decided to release my SEO tool to the world. In mid 2012, I launched "*SEO Meta Manager*" for Shopify (http://SEOMetaManager.com). Within 90 days, SEO Meta Manager became the best selling SEO app in the Shopify app store. For a time, SEO Meta Manager was the most popular application in the entire Shopify app store.

I am a huge fan of Shopify.com, and I really enjoy SEO. When coupled together, I have seen some amazing results. My purpose for writing this book is to help business owners, like yourself, get the most out of the Shopify platform, and leverage SEO in order to grow your business.

This book provides information on SEO best practices and core principals that I use everyday to produce results for my clients.

Now is the time for you to start building your Shopify Empire.

Dominate search results. Sell more. Change your world.

LET'S DO THIS!

-- Josh Highland

Disclaimer

The thoughts and opinions expressed in this book are those of the author and do not represent Shopify.

---

1. UNDERSTANDING SEO

Take a moment and think, *how many times have I used a search engine like Google or Bing to find something online? How often do I find what I am looking for within the first few results on the first page? How did Google know which results to show first? How do I get my site listed in the top results?* The answer to all of these questions is **SEO**. SEO is an acronym for *Search Engine Optimization*. In a nutshell, SEO is the practice of getting your website's pages listed and ranked highly in search engine results.

Why SEO Matters

If you have an online store powered by Shopify, you have something that you want to sell. To sell your products, you need people visiting your site. Herein lies one of the major problems of online storeowners around the world, *"How do I increase traffic to my store?"*

Most people use search engines to find things online that they are looking for. If someone were to search Google for a product that you are selling it would be optimal for your store to be listed in the results that are returned. If a link to your store is not returned in the results, the user will not be able to easily discover your site. Moreover, even if your store was found in the search results, users typically only click the top few links in the results page.

In June of 2013, Chakita.com, a well-known ad marketing agency, released a study on the value of Google search result positioning. (http://chitika.com/google-positioning-value)

Google Result Page Rank	Traffic Share
1	33.5 %
2	17.6 %
3	11.4 %
4	8.1 %
5	6.1 %
6	4.4 %
7	3.5 %
8	3.1 %
9	2.6 %
10	2.4 %

Figure 1-1

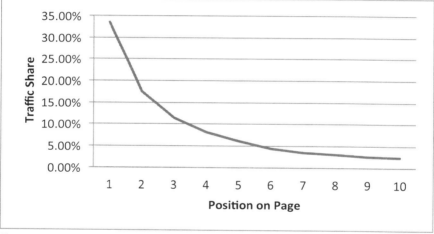

Figure 1-2

The data showed that over 62% of users click one of the top three results, with 76% clicking one of the top five results. However, more than one third, 33.5% of users, click on the number one result.

The study also showed that 91.5% of all Google traffic is generated by the first page of results (Figure 1-3). The traffic data past the first page shows a steep decline (Figure 1-4). The second page of Google search results received less than 5% of all traffic. Only one person in 100 (1.1%) made it to the third page of results, while one in 250 users (0.4%) clicked on links from the 4th page of results.

Result Page	% of Traffic
Page 1	91.5 %
Page 2	4.8 %
Page 3	1.1 %
Page 4	0.4 %

Figure 1-3

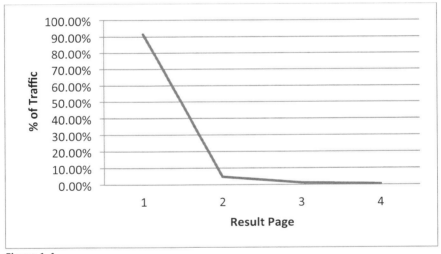

Figure 1-4

The study found that most users click the first link on the first Search Engine Results Page (SERP). This means that the top rank carries the most authority and user confidence. Google does a great job of bringing relevant data to the top of its results pages. As users we have become conditioned to trust that the top search results will hold what we are searching for, and more often than not, it does.

To surmise, having your Shopify store rank highly in Google searches will mean more clicks into your site, which results in more visitors, which then translates into more sales. The goal of this book is to provide you with the skills you need to rise in the ranks and capture top search engine result positions.

Algorithms - Ingredients and Recipes

Google and Bing return impressive results when you search for a subject. *But how do they know what websites are about? How do they know which websites to list first?* Each search engine has its own special set of rules that help it determine how to rank websites. Technically speaking, those rules are called *algorithms*. You can think of these algorithms as secret recipes that search engines follow when ranking and listing websites.

Search engines continuously scan the Internet, following website links, and collecting information on everything they find. Think of the information that they collect as ingredients. The secret to higher search engine rankings is to make sure that your website contains all of the ingredients that the search engines need to complete their secret recipe. It sounds easy right? It would be if the search engines told us the recipes they were following, but they do not.

Now, let us think of another closely guarded recipe, Coca-Cola Classic. If you called the Coke corporate offices and asked them for the recipe, you would not get very far. Their formula is what makes Coke unique. Similarly, search engine algorithms are closely guarded secrets, with only the provider knowing the exact recipe. If the exact algorithm was know, it would be easy to add all of the required data to your site, and in effect manipulate the search results. If this happened, it would lead to low quality websites making their way to the top of the results, and ultimately people would stop using that search engine because the results would be "spammy", poor and irrelevant.

Moving Targets

We do not know Coke's exact formula but you can look at the label on a bottle and see the major ingredients. Coke must disclose this information for many reasons, and we can use the ingredient list to gain limited insight as to what is needed to make Coke Classic taste delicious. If we tried hard enough, we may be able to reverse engineer the exact proportions of ingredients on the list and unlock the secrets of Coke.

Since search engine rankings are so valuable, SEO experts conduct countless experiments to reverse engineer the search algorithms used by Google and Bing. By making tiny adjustments SEO experts are able to monitor what works and what does not. Over time these experts slowly begin to crack the algorithms. Given enough time, the algorithms would be completely unlocked. Google and Bing know this, so they routinely change their search formula, which creates moving targets. Unlike Coca-Cola, which is famous in part for its consistent taste, search engines need to continuously make changes to their product and "recipe" to keep up with trends, and thereby deliver the best results to their users.

Google has made considerable changes to their algorithm over the last few years. The most recent major update was dubbed "*Hummingbird*." Google named it as such due to the nature of a hummingbird – fast, nimble, elegant – able to change direction in an instant.

The major focus of the Hummingbird update was to support the way people use search engines today. Consumers tend to use longer more specific search strings. Typically, users are not just searching for the term "Bicycle" if they want to buy a bike. Instead, they are likely to perform a more specific search such as "Mountain bikes for sale." Because Google knows where you are located, the search results would be tailored to bike shops in the area that you live. Powering these changes are mobile phones, location tracking software, voice recognition software, and increasing user sophistication.

In the past, there were unscrupulous techniques that made it easy to rank your site at the top of the listings for specific search phrases. Hummingbird and other algorithm changes are now actively looking for unethical SEO behaviors, and punishing sites that use dishonest methods to advance in the ranks. In some cases, these sites are completely removed from search listings – SEO suicide.

Despite the fact that search engine algorithms are constantly evolving, there are many best practices that search engines look for and reward. Later in this book we will explore these factors, explain how to implement them, and show you how to measure SEO success for your Shopify store.

Expectations

Making it to the top of the search engine results is not a quick process. In most cases it a slow progression of gains until you make the front page of Google. Some market niches are more difficult to break into than others. If you sell hats and are hoping to rank for the search phrase "Baseball hats," it will take much more effort than someone selling "Men's hair pomade," as the market for hats is more saturated and difficult to breach. In 2008, I actually sold men's hair pomade via a Shopify store. I was able to make it to the front page of Google within two months using the methods described in this book. Making it to the front page of Google more than tripled my business.

It is crucial to understand that SEO is a marathon, not a sprint. It may be possible to make large gains relatively quickly, but in most cases it takes several weeks or months before search engines start to rank your shop higher. Do not be discouraged by this. Improving search ranking may take time and effort, but the rewards are worth the investment.

If you met a person who was out of shape, but expected to become a vision of health after one day in the gym, it would be obvious that the person was delusional. We all know that getting in shape is a long process, and is difficult. Despite being challenging, the activities associated with healthy living yield profound results over time. You must think of SEO in the same way. Implementing SEO changes and mitigating existing SEO issues is time consuming, and the effects are not visible immediately, however the end results are absolutely worth it.

I like the analogy of SEO and fitness a lot. Both require work, dedication and the right mindset to achieve results. Similarly, in both cases it may be beneficial to get a kick-start by hiring a personal trainer, or in the case of SEO, an SEO consultant.

If you met a personal trainer that told you they could take you from being overweight to an Olympic competitor over night, or even in a month, it would raise some red flags. The effort-to-time ratio is all wrong. If you choose to hire an SEO expert to assist you, and they promise you a top rank position, or first page positioning within x amount of time – run away quickly! Guaranteed position placement is almost always a sign of a scam or unethical activities that violate Google's policies. If you need help, look for SEO consultants with demonstrated experience and an existing client portfolio. Shopify makes this easy to do with Shopify Certified Experts - http://experts.shopify.com.

Shopify Experts are pre-screened and have demonstrated knowledge of the Shopify platform. Due to their expertise, they are uniquely suited to help their clients become successful. If you would like to hire my company, NewLeaf Labs, we are listed at - http://experts.shopify.com/newleaf-labs.

2. BUILDING THE FOUNDATION

"You never get a second chance to make a good first impression."

-- Will Rogers

You are using Shopify because you have products that you want to sell. To sell products you need more than great SEO. You can use every SEO and marketing tactic in this book, rank highly in search engine results, and not sell a single thing if you do not have user trust and authority.

Aside from pricing, user trust is what separates your store from other stores that sell similar products. Factors such as domain name, web site interface, graphics, product photos, product descriptions, and check out experience all contribute to user confidence.

If you were going on an interview for your dream job, you would most likely take a shower, comb your hair, and put on a business suit. Why is that? We engage in these processes to make a positive first impression with a potential employer. It is often suggested that one should, "dress for the job you want, not the job you have." We put our best foot forward with the hopes that our appearance will increase trust and show that we are a fit for the job.

It is essential to think of every person that visits your Shopify store as a potential customer. Those visitors begin to form an opinion about your store from the moment they view your listing on a search result page (SERP). If your page information looks good in the SERP, a person may click through to your site. Once your page loads, visitors determine within seconds if your store looks interesting and trust worthy. If a user has little trust in your site, they click the back button in their browser and go to another listing, your competitor's site. Despite having better SEO and ranking higher in Google you lost the sale. Not good.

The following chapter will help your Shopify store gain user confidence and help convert visitors into customers. Google also values sites that present themselves as professional. Getting your site in order is one of the simplest forms of SEO.

Domain Names

By default every Shopify store comes with a URL (web address) of: *YourStoreName.myshopify.com,* where YourStoreName is the name of your Shopify account. It is possible to launch your store with a URL like YourStoreName.myshopify.com, but take a moment and think of the following.

Which link would you click first?

> runningShoes.myshopify.com
> RunningShoeOutlet.com

How about

> cic2.myshopify.com
> CustomiPhoneCases.com

Most of you probably picked the links that did NOT contain ".myshopify.com." Shoppers tend to place more trust in companies that have their own domain name.

Keywords in a domain name also help to increase authority. A site named "CustomiPhoneCases.com" is most likely not selling dog toys. As the name suggests, they are selling Custom iPhone cases. Key worded domains do well, but can become a niche sticking point in the future if the iPhone is no longer in production, or if you want to start selling other products.

I believe that companies should own their domains names. Meaning that "Quilts by Kate" should have a corresponding domain name "QuiltsByKate.com" or "KatesQuilts.com." Marketing material also looks more professional with a custom domain name, as do email addresses.

Which has more authority and looks more professional?

Support@CustomiPhoneCases.com
CustomiPhoneCasesSupport@yahoo.com

Another argument in favor of a custom domain name is portability. Shopify is an amazing platform, but if for some reason you need to change ecommerce providers in the future, it is easy to do with a custom domain, and very difficult to do if you are still using a ".myshopify.com" domain – Not that you would ever want to leave Shopify!

HOW TO USE A CUSTOM DOMAIN NAME WITH SHOPIFY

Shopify makes it easy to use a custom domain name with your store. The quickest and easiest way is to buy your domain through Shopify's Admin Dashboard. It is relatively straightforward and Shopify does all the setup work for you.

To buy a domain name for your Shopify store:

1. Go to Settings → Domains in your admin panel.

2. Click the "Buy a domain" button in the upper right hand corner.

3. Pick the "Register a new domain" option.

4. A new window will pop up. Type in the domain name that you would like and pick an extension (.com, .net, etc.)

5. Click the "Check availability" button. If this domain is available, Shopify will register and process it for you (Figure 2-1).

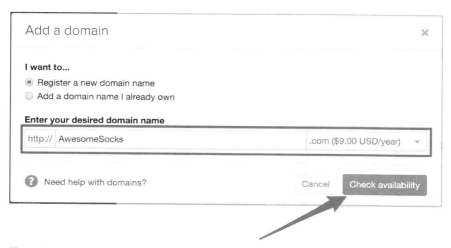

Figure 2-1

If you already own a domain name, you are able to use it with Shopify. The instructions are slightly more involved and require DNS configuration changes with your domain registrar, but it is still fairly easy. You are able to find full instructions on how to configure your own domain name with Shopify here: http://docs.shopify.com/manual/settings/domains

WWW VS NON-WWW DOMAINS

Google and other search engines are very particular when it comes to domain names. Google sees http://www.YourStore.com and http://YourStore.com as completely separate sites. Both URLs most likely go to the same place, but to Google one of the sites is full of duplicate content and appears as a clone of the other site.

Google tends to not include sites with duplicate content in search results. The situation deepens when other sites and social media users start linking to your site and products. Some people will include the "www", and some will not.

The easiest way to avoid this problem is to add both the WWW and Non-WWW to your list of Shopify domains, and then select the version that you would like to use for your store (Figure 2-2 and 2-3). I prefer the non-WWW version, but that is completely up to you.

Domain	Status	
merchcon.myshopify.com	OK	
merchconnectioninc.com	OK	🗑
www.merchconnectioninc.com	OK	🗑

Figure 2-2

Primary domain

www.merchconnectioninc.com ⬍

☑ Redirect all traffic to this domain
   This will redirect traffic from all your domains to the single primary domain.

Figure 2-3

Now when someone goes to the WWW version of your store, or the non-WWW version, they will always get redirected to the right URL. This simple change can have large impacts on your SEO and brand building efforts.

Themes

The interface of your Shopify store is controlled by a theme. A theme is a bundle of graphics and code that gives your store a specific look and feel. The outward appearance of your site is a significantly large and critical component of creating user trust. Shopify knows this fact, and goes to great lengths to make stunning themes available to their users.

THE SHOPIFY THEME STORE

Shopify has an entire theme store filled with brilliant themes for you to choose - http://themes.shopify.com (Figure 2-4). Basic themes are usually free, and premium themes can cost as much as $200 each. Do not think of a theme purchase as an expense; rather think of it as an investment in your business. I highly suggest that you take the time to look over all of the available themes.

Figure 2-4

With an entire theme store to choose from, picking the right theme for your site may be overwhelming. Here are some tips that I give my clients.

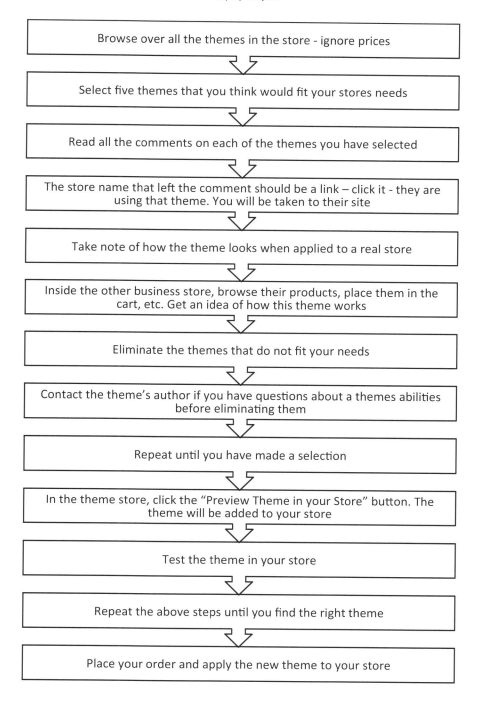

Browse over all the themes in the store - ignore prices

Select five themes that you think would fit your stores needs

Read all the comments on each of the themes you have selected

The store name that left the comment should be a link – click it - they are using that theme. You will be taken to their site

Take note of how the theme looks when applied to a real store

Inside the other business store, browse their products, place them in the cart, etc. Get an idea of how this theme works

Eliminate the themes that do not fit your needs

Contact the theme's author if you have questions about a themes abilities before eliminating them

Repeat until you have made a selection

In the theme store, click the "Preview Theme in your Store" button. The theme will be added to your store

Test the theme in your store

Repeat the above steps until you find the right theme

Place your order and apply the new theme to your store

Do you think that $150 or $200 is too much to pay for a theme? The following statements may change your mind:

- Studies have shown that within seconds of visiting a site, based on appearance, visitors decide to stay and shop, or leave

- You are running a business, the cost of a theme may be tax deductible

- Attractive sites sell more products. More sales mean more profits. A quality theme will pay for itself

- Custom Shopify themes typically cost between $1500 - $5000, and may include charges for upgrades and enhancements

HIRE A THEME DESIGNER

If you are unable to find a theme in the theme store that fits your needs, you may need to hire a theme designer. Do not worry about looking high and low to find a Shopify Theme Designer, Shopify has that covered. As part of the Shopify Experts program, Shopify certifies expert designers, and makes it easier for you to contact them - http://experts.shopify.com/designers. To become a design expert, one must be vetted by Shopify. This process ensures a high level of craftsmanship and knowledge on the subject of Shopify themes. Many of the themes available in the theme store were created by Shopify Design Experts.

Be prepared to spend a fair amount of money on a custom theme. A custom theme can cost around $3000 to create, and may cost more if changes are needed in the future. Before hiring a designer, look at their work and tell them what you liked, and did not like with the themes you saw in the theme store. This will help guide the designer in creating a theme for your store.

MAKING YOUR OWN THEME

Making your own theme is by far more complicated than buying one from the store, or having a designer create one for you. Only venture down this path if you are an experienced web developer, and would like a new challenge. By experienced web developer, I do not mean that you dabble with making websites. After all, you are building a business, and that should be your main focus.

Now, if you are a web ninja, and you like to know how things work from top to bottom (I know I do), it is possible to create your own theme, or to modify one that you have downloaded from the theme store. Shopify themes are made up of HTML, JavaScript, CSS, Graphics, and are powered by a markup language called *Liquid*.

> **If any of those words sounded foreign to you, you are better off buying a theme – trust me.**

Shopify does an amazing job at helping people who want to create their own themes. They have created extensive documentation on theme creation best practices - http://docs.shopify.com/themes

CHANGING YOUR STORES THEME

Shopify allows several themes to be installed in a store at a time. Switching between themes only requires a few clicks of the mouse. In most cases you should be able to switch between themes with minimal hassle (Figure 2-5), typically only a few settings changes are needed. Shopify also allows you to preview un-published themes. Previewing themes allows you, the store admin, to make simple setting updates and experience the new theme in your store before making it visible to your customers (Figure 2-6).

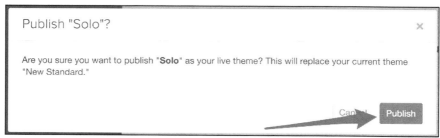

Figure 2-5

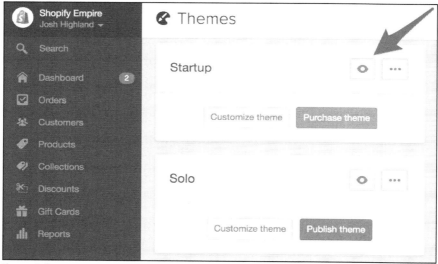

Figure 2-6

3. STRUCTURED FOR SUCCESS

"Organizing is what you do before you do something, so that when you do it, it is not all mixed up."

-- A. A. Milne

Structure – search engines and customers LOVE it!

When a person searches Google and finds your site, odds are they will land on a product page. It is important to understand how your product pages relate to the other pages on your site. If the page they are on is not the exact product they want, they should be able to quickly navigate to another, similar product. Visitors should quickly be able to know where they are, and how to traverse your site. Your site should be intuitive, with no learning required.

As Internet users, we have all visited sites that were confusing to navigate and poorly laid out. Instead of fumbling our way through the site, we press the back button in our web browser and move on to the next search result. Visitors have short attention spans and want the information they are looking for delivered quickly. The title of Steve Krug's classic book on web usability sums it up best, *"Don't Make Me Think."* (http://www.sensible.com/dmmt.html)

In the physical world, before the construction of a building is started, a plan is needed. The plan shows how the different components of the building work together. It is much easier to make changes on paper before construction starts. Your site may only exist online, but you still need a plan if you are going to build a successful store. Before you can make a plan you need to understand all of the elements that you have available to work with.

The Structural Elements of a Shopify Store

Shopify is a great platform to work with, and comes equipped with all of the structural elements that you need to build an exceptional site, you just need to understand what they are and what they are best used for.

- **Home page** - This is the page that loads when you enter your sites URL into a web browser. Think of this as the front door or lobby to your store.

- **Collections** - Groupings of products. Manually defined or based on parameters. Usually they are delineated by vendor, style, or price (Example: Products under $10, or Men's Shirts).

- **Products** - These pages list your product information and showcase the items you are selling. These pages should include *"add to cart"* and *"check out"* options.

- **Pages** – Pages are free form and allow you to enter content that is not directly tied to a product. (Examples: About Us, Return Policies, Contact Information).

- **Blog Posts** - Blog Posts make up the content of a blog. Blog posts are an effective way to add content to your site. (Example: "10 things every woman needs in her purse" or "This week's sale items").

UNDERSTANDING COLLECTIONS

Envision a department store. The store is divided into logical groupings that assist customers in navigating the store without feeling overwhelmed by all of the products.

Example:
- Women's clothing
- Women's shoes
- Men's clothing
- Housewares
- Bedding

THE COLLECTIONS YOU NEED

Collections help tell the story of your products to a visitor. How do you want your customers to find your products? By brand, by type, by price?

If you were selling shoes online, the following collections may make sense:

By Type:
- Running Shoes
- Basketball Shoes
- Tennis Shoes
- Skateboard Shoes

By Brand:
- Nike
- Reebok
- Adidas
- Converse

Other Categories:
- On Sale
- Best Sellers

The collections listed above give the user a lot of variety on how to navigate your site, while still considering how a user may want to browse your products. Someone may be in the market for new running shoes, so they would go to the running shoe collection. If someone is a fan of Nike shoes, they may want to go directly to the Nike shoes.

Collections are very powerful, but with great power comes great responsibility. Just because you can slice your store into a hundred different collections does not mean you should. Your collections should not overwhelm a visitor, but gently guide the visitor to the product they are looking for. I once saw a shop that had a collection for every possible combination of products. They had almost as many categories as they had products to sell. Collections based on color, size, style, shape, brand, season, interest, and the like. It sounds great on paper, but in reality it was just cluttered and confusing. In many cases less is more. You can always expand if you feel that you need more collections to tell the story of your shop. Start by creating categories that encompass large portions of your products. Keep the category names something general, yet descriptive of the products.

Examples of simple and well-organized categories:
collections/Nike
collections/Reebok
collections/Adidas
collections/Converse
collections/Running-Shoes
collections/Basketball-Shoes
collections/Tennis-Shoes
collections/Skateboard-Shoes

Examples of categories that are too specific:

collections/Nike-Shoes-Size-11
collections/Nike-Shoes-Size-10
collections/Nike-Shoes-Size-9
collections/Nike-Shoes-Basket-Ball
collections/Nike-Shoes-Running
collections/Nike-Shoes-Skateboard
collections/White-Nike-Shoes
collections/Black-Nike-Shoes
collections/Brown-Nike-Shoes
collections/Black-Nike-Shoes-Skateboard-size-11
collections/Black-Nike-Shoes-Skateboard-size-10
collections/Black-Nike-Shoes-Skateboard-size-9

THE PAGES YOU NEED

To figure out what pages your store needs, think of the customer. As a customer, what information would you want to see about this store? Keep in mind that pages are not meant to list products, or act as a blog. Pages are for information that does not change often. Having meaningful content on these pages increases trust for both users and search engines.

Common pages that every store should have:

About Us - A page about the company. Why do you sell what you sell? Tell users about the things that set you apart from your competitors. What is your competitive advantage?

Contact Us - How your customers can get in touch with you if they have questions.

FAQs - Frequently asked questions about your products / services / site.

Return Policy - Information on how product returns are handled.

<u>WHAT TO BLOG ABOUT</u>

First of all, every store should have a blog. Blog posts are a great way to generate new content, and search engines love sites that add new content on a regular basis. You may think that you do not have enough time to blog, that it is too difficult, or that you do not have anything interesting to say. You are wrong.

If you are selling something, you have something to tell people. As a shop owner you should be able to answer these questions:

- Who are you?
- Why did you choose the name of your business?
- Why did you choose to sell these products?
- Why should someone buy from you?
- What makes your products different?
- What are your products made from? Why?
- What is the latest technology begin used in your market space?
- What is your return policy?
- Has anyone famous bought something from you?
- What are your most popular products?
- What are the newest products in your store?

The options for blog posts are almost endless. Blogging does not have to be an epic task, and blog posts do not always have to be award-winning works of art. As long as they are genuine, original, and consistent, you will be in good shape.

Blog posts should be:

- Interesting
- Informative
- Contain key phrases that people will search for

- Posted on a regular basis

Making your blog posts interesting and informative should go without saying. Remember that your blog posts should add value to your site. If you need help creating content, I suggest hiring a content writer.

Writing good posts is important, and content will always be king. However, a regular publishing schedule is a key to success. I recommend that you take 30 minutes each week and write a new blog post. Making blogging a part of your routine will help you develop the habit of adding new content to your site. Search engines like Google look for content freshness, as it is an indicator that the shop is alive and well. Fresh content also gives people something to talk about, something to link to, something to share on social media (via social share buttons), and something to comment on. Google LOVES popular sites, and popularity is measured by how many people are linking to and talking about a site. Later in the book we will talk about writing *"link bait"*, content that encourages people to link to your site.

If you sell sports memorabilia, blogging about how cute your dog is – not a good idea. Blogging about the Dodgers making it to the MLB playoffs – good idea. Blogging about how the Dodgers made it to the playoffs, including a picture of your dog wearing a Dodgers jersey, made specifically for dogs, and sold on your site – GREAT IDEA!

Executing the plan

Now that you know what pages, collections and blog posts you need, the next step is to create them. It is best to focus on your stores content before worrying about how it looks. Shopify makes it easy to modify your shop's theme. You can spend a lot of time making your site look pixel perfect, but without good content, it is going to be hard to get customers to buy your products, or have search engines rank you highly. Take the time to organize and input your products, collections, pages and blog posts in Shopify. I have seen dramatic changes in search engine ranking and customer purchasing behavior, simply by organizing a sites content into a simple and understandable format.

Navigation

Once you have added content to your site, you need to update your site's navigation menus. Site navigation is controlled by *"link lists."* Link lists are, as the name suggests, lists of links. Clicking *"Navigation"* on the left side of the Shopify Admin will open the Link lists manager (Figure 3-1).

In this example, we have linked lists for *"Main Menu"* and *"Footer"*

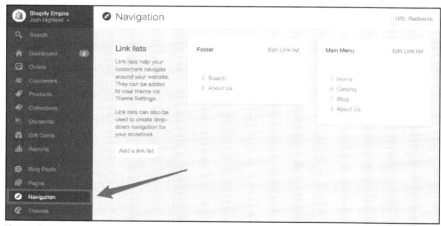

Figure 3-1

- Clicking on the *"Edit Link list"* button for the *"Main Menu"* link list shows the links and the order they will appear in the main navigation area of your site

- You can use the control handle on the left side of a link to reorder the links in the list

- Clicking *"Add another link"* will add another link to the list (Figure 3-2)

- Each link needs a name, this is the name that is displayed to your users, and search engines

- Select where this link will point. In this example, I have chosen *"collection"*

- Select the collection that this link should be pointed to. Clicking the *"Select a collection"* drop down will open a dialog window that will list all of your shops collections

- Click the *"Save"* button when you are done

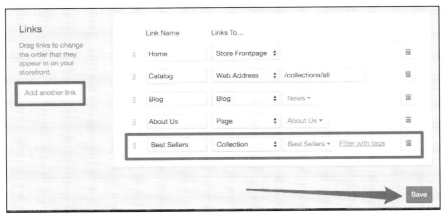

Figure 3-2

After updating the Main Menu linked list, your theme should reflect the changes that you made.

> Note:
> Each theme is different, so consult the instructions that came with your theme, or ask the developer that made your theme how to do this.

Remove the Barriers

I have seen a number of Shopify stores that require users to create an account before they are allowed to buy anything (Figure 3-3). There are even some Shopify apps that prevent people from checking out if they do not have enough items in their cart (http://apps.shopify.com/minimum-orders)

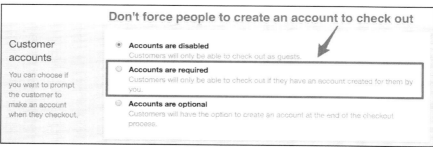

Figure 3-3

As a business owner, I understand the importance of capturing information on who your customers are, but from a consumer standpoint I find it very frustrating when shop owners do this. There have been several occasions where I have left a site due to the sign up or check out process. In most cases, I just place my order on another site.

Over the years I have even seen some sites that require visitors to register or create an account BEFORE they can even browse the products in the store. This is one of the most harmful things you can do for SEO and customer conversions.

You have an online store because you want to sell things. You are reading this book because you want to attract people to your store. Once you have people visiting your site, you want them to buy things. Remove the barriers! Let visitors browse your products freely. Remember, not all visitors are real people. Search engines like Google and Bing have computer programs called "spiders" that go out and crawl the "web." These programs look at sites, collect information from them, and then add them to the search engine index. The search index is where search results are drawn from. If your store cannot freely be searched by these programs, it will be difficult to get listed by the search engines, and in turn, hard for you to rank in search engine results.

Once you get people to your site, and they are actively adding items to their cart, the check out process should be simple. The easier you can make the check out experience, the less time the customer will have to think about the purchase they are making, and if they really need the items they are buying. This is why Amazon.com patented the "1-Click" checkout concept. Shopify has a nice check out process, and allows the shopping cart pages to be controlled by themes. Make sure your store's cart page is easy to use, and encourages users to check out with the least amount of steps.

Once the user reaches the checkout page, they need to pay for their order. In my experience I have found that offering several payment methods has been very beneficial for my clients. Along with credit cards you should have PayPal enabled as a payment method. PayPal is a secure and popular payment method that many people prefer over credit cards. If someone wants to give you money, do not limit them.

The Fundamentals Are Foundational

So far we have covered how to create a professional appearance, how to work with themes, the basic content types in Shopify, and how to structure your sites content. You now have the knowledge and resources to build a nice online store powered by Shopify. If you need to, go back and cover this material again. If you like, take the time and adjust your shop. Basic changes can have the largest SEO impact on a site. It is highly important to understand the fundamental components of your shop. The following chapters are going to revolve around the fine-tuning of those elements.

4. TYPES OF SEO

"If it isn't on Google, it doesn't exist."

-- Jimmy Wales, co-founder of Wikipedia

By now you should have a beautiful Shopify store. Hopefully you already have some customers, and you have begun appearing in Google search results when you search for your brand name. The goal now is to improve your shop's ranking in search engine results, and in turn, increase the number of visitors landing on your site, ultimately converting those visitors into paying customers.

SEO efforts typically fall into one of two categories, on-site optimization, and off-site optimization. On-site optimizations are changes that you can make directly to your shop that have a positive SEO impact. Off-site optimization focuses on positive SEO impacts, contributed by other websites. As you can imagine, on-site optimization is easier to address because you are in control of your site. Off-site changes remain more difficult and are typically marketing related.

On-site SEO optimization involves making changes to your shop's theme and modifying settings. Generally on-site SEO problems are easy to address and can be made right from the Shopify admin dashboard. There are also several apps in the Shopify app store specifically designed to help with on-site SEO.

Off-site SEO optimization helps raise awareness of your site. Usually it involves collaborating with other websites and services.

For example, guest blogging, contest hosting and social media participation.

Optimization vs. Marketing

Search Engine Optimization (SEO) and Search Engine Marketing (SEM) are terms that are commonly used interchangeably. SEO and SEM are similar to each other in that they both drive traffic to your site, however the method by which that traffic is achieved is markedly different. Essentially, Search Engine Marketing is the purchase of ad space online.

Pay Per Click (PPC) SEM strategies through services like Google Adwords enhance the visibility of your site and products by injecting your sites listing into search results. Depending on the search results you target, PPC campaigns can be costly. When you stop paying for the ads, your site disappears from the sponsored section of the search results. For this reason alone, it is important for Shopify storeowners to have an organic SEO strategy. SEO produces sustained search engine listings without a reoccurring cost. Pay Per Click campaigns are still a good tool for gaining visitors to your store, but before investing in PPC, your site should be optimized to convert visitors into buying customers. This includes having a good theme, product descriptions, and engaging product photos.

From my experience, organic SEO efforts result in the most sustainable growth and the highest return on investment for business owners. The remaining content of this book will focus directly on organic SEO. If you would like to learn more about Search Engine Marketing and PPC campaigns, I suggest reading *"Ultimate Guide to Pay-Per-Click Advertising"* by Richard Stokes (http://www.adgooroo.com/resources/ultimate-guide).

5. ON-SITE OPTIMIZATION

"In general, webmasters can improve the rank of their sites by creating high-quality sites that users will want to use and share."

-- *Google Webmasters Website*
*(*https://support.google.com/webmasters/answer/34432*)*

As we discussed at the start of this book, search engines like Google and Bing do not disclose the way by which they rank sites. They do, however, give us a list of major items that they look for. SEO is a game of small victories and fine-tuning, and any time that a search engine company gives us hints on how to rank better, we should apply them to our site. Always remember – simple changes can have dramatic SEO results.

Content is King

If you take one thing away from this book, let it be this: *WRITE GOOD CONTENT*. This will have more impact on your SEO performance than anything else in this book. Without solid content on your site, all other SEO tactics are futile. Quality content is the foundation that modern SEO is built upon.

In the past, Google and other search engines simply matched patterns that users searched for. If you wanted a specific page to be found in a search, you had to include the exact phrase multiple times on the page, a practice known as "keyword stuffing." Through this practice, SEO experts became very good at manipulating search result listings. This led to a lot of low quality content at the top of the search engines result pages. Most of the content was horrible to read, and not useful.

Google latest search update, *"Hummingbird,"* has made it almost impossible to rank highly through Keyword stuffing. In the modern SEO world, keywords still play an important role, but they are not nearly as important as they were in the past. Today, Google takes intent, synonyms, and context into account when ranking sites. Google has also gotten very clever and started looking for words and phrases **not** used on the page. Basically Google is reading between the lines, and looking for phrases and words that an expert on a subject would or would not include in their content. Because of this simple change, stuffing keywords and key phrases into content, as was done in the past, does not help you rank better and may in fact damage your SEO efforts.

Ask yourself

"Would this content look out of place, or sound strange if it was in a printed magazine?"

If your answer is "yes"– you know that your content needs help. Your content should be crafted for your visitors, not for search engines. It needs to read well, and have no visible signs of added key phrases intended to elevate page rank.

If you want to rank in the top 10 search results, your content should also deliver value that other sites in the top results do not. Your sites content must be unique and noteworthy.

I am not suggesting that you should not have specific keywords or phrases that you are trying to rank for. By all means, you need to choose what phrases you are targeting and go after them, but do it in a natural manner. Always think of your customers first. Use the language of your specific industry and focus on the readability and value of content. This goes for all content that you write –

your home page, your product descriptions, your "contact us" page, the "about us" page, and every blog post you make. EVERYTHING.

Understanding Meta Tags and Meta Data

Meta data is information about information. Meta tags are pieces of computer code that contain meta data. Simply put, meta tags contain descriptive data about your sites pages. Meta tags are found within the "*head tags*" of your site (<head>...</head>), and typically found in the "*theme.liquid*" file of a Shopify theme. Meta Data is used by search engines to help determine what a webpage is about, and how to list it in search results. Meta Data is not visible to your sites visitors, but is essential for SEO purposes.

Title, Description, Keywords - The Meta Data Trinity

There are many meta tags available for sites, but when someone mentions a site's "*meta tags*" or "*meta data*" in a SEO context, they are typically talking about a pages Title, Meta Description and Meta Keywords – The big three.

The Title Tag

When it comes to on-page SEO tuning, the title tag is one of the most import things to focus on. Search Engines directly use the title tag in search engine result pages (Figure 5-1). The page title is the first thing about your site that users see on a search result page. Users can also see this text in their Bookmarks/Favorites menu after they save the page to their web browser's bookmarks.

Figure 5-1

The title denotes what a page is about and is highly valued by search engines. Therefore, this is where you should place the most important keywords you are optimizing the page for. Here is where the art of SEO comes into practice. You need to truthfully describe what the page is about, but at the same time include the key phrases (keywords) that people would search for to find the page. To complicate things even further, it is recommended that you do this in 70 characters or less (and you thought twitter was restrictive!)

Uniqueness is also an important factor for titles. If your site contains several pages with the same title, Google may have a hard time listing them properly. In some cases, Google will only keep the most popular page of your site, and exclude all of the pages with duplicate titles, something that we definitely do not want.

The title tag should:

- Be 70 characters or less
- Describe the content of the page
- Contain descriptive keywords
- Be unique per page

THE HOME PAGE TITLE

Setting the title for your site's home page can be done by navigating to the *"Settings → General Settings"* in the Shopify admin panel. From this page you are able to update your shop's home page title (Figure 5-2).

Figure 5-2

TITLES FOR COLLECTIONS, PRODUCTS, PAGES AND THE REST

In the Shopify Admin for your store, you will see a set of *"Search Engines"* fields near the bottom of any content page (product, collection, page, or blog article). By default the *"Page title"* field is populated with the title of the object you are working with (Figure 5-3). Updating this field will alter the title that search engines use when listing this page.

Figure 5-3

CAN YOUR THEME SUPPORT SEO TITLES?

To take advantage of this data, your shop's theme needs to use the *"page_title"* variable for the value of the title tag. You can check this by looking at the *"theme.liquid"* file in your theme bundle (Figure 5-4).

> **If you are uncomfortable with Shopify theme code, you may want to have a Shopify expert help you with this.**

In the Shopify admin panel:
- Click *"Themes"*
- Then click the *"..."* button next to your theme
- Select *"Edit HTML/CSS"* from the drop down menu
- Click on *"theme.liquid"* in the code editor
- Look for *"{{ page_title }}"* in the code

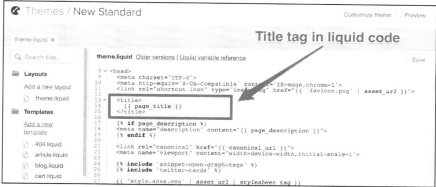

Figure 5-4

The Description Meta Tag

The description meta tag is another important on-page item that search engines look at closely when ranking your site. The meta description is not seen by the users when they visit your site, however, search engines like Google display the meta description on search result pages (Figure 5-5). In Google's case, the meta description is displayed below the title of the page.

Figure 5-5

Meta descriptions help search engines and users quickly understand what a page is about. The description is a brief explanation of what a user will find on that page and why it matters. This is where you sell the users on why they should click into your site.

Your description needs to be something compelling, truthful, unique, and contain the key phrases that people would use to find this page. You need to do this in 160 characters or less (only 20 more characters than a tweet). Do not worry; it is not as hard as it sounds once you get the hang of it!

THE HOME PAGE DESCRIPTION

Setting the meta description for your site's home page can be done by navigating to *"Settings → General Settings"* in the Shopify admin. From this page you should be able to update your shops homepage description (Figure 5-6).

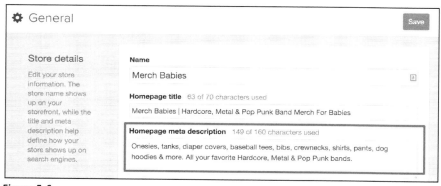

Figure 5-6

DESCRIPTIONS FOR COLLECTIONS, PRODUCTS, PAGES AND THE REST

Navigate to almost any page in the Shopify admin and you will see a set of *"Search Engines"* fields near the bottom of the page. By default the *"Meta description"* is populated with the body text of the object you are working with (product, collection, page, blog, article). Updating this field will alter the description that search engines will see for this page, your customers will still see the body text that you set above (Figure 5-7).

Figure 5-7

CAN YOUR THEME SUPPORT SEO DESCRIPTIONS?

> **If you are uncomfortable with Shopify theme code, you may want to have a Shopify expert help you with this.**

To take advantage of this data, your shop's theme needs to be programmed to use the "*page_description*" liquid variable, for the value of the meta description field. You can check this by looking at the "*theme.liquid*" file in your theme bundle (Figure 5-8).

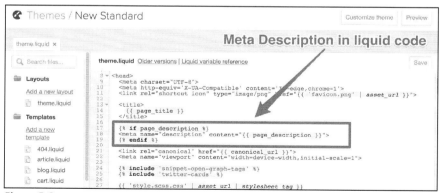

Figure 5-8

The Keyword Meta Tag

The keyword meta tag has an interesting history. It was originally used to store words and phrases that described how the site should be listed in search results. For a long time, this was a very valuable piece of SEO data. Yet, over time, this was highly abused by people trying to game the system in order to rank higher. It was so abused that Google now officially ignores the keyword meta tag.

The following are questions and answers taken from Google's blog for site owners - http://googlewebmastercentral.blogspot.com/2009/09/google-does-not-use-keywords-meta-tag.html

Q: Does Google ever use the "keywords" meta tag in its web search ranking?

A: In a word, no. Google does sell a Google Search Appliance, and that product has the ability to match meta tags, which could include the keywords meta tag. But that's an enterprise search appliance that is completely separate from our main web search. Our web search (the well-known search at Google.com that hundreds of millions of people use each day) disregards keyword meta tags completely. They simply don't have any effect in our search ranking at present.

Q: Why doesn't Google use the keywords meta tag?

A: About a decade ago, search engines judged pages only on the content of web pages, not any so-called "off-page" factors such as the links pointing to a web page. In those days, keyword meta tags quickly became an area where someone could stuff often-irrelevant keywords without typical visitors ever seeing those keywords. Because the keywords meta tag was so often abused, many years ago Google began disregarding the keywords meta tag.

So what does this mean for us? Essentially – Do not worry about the keywords meta tag. Shopify is aware of Google not valuing Keywords meta tags, and does not include them in the customizable SEO fields.

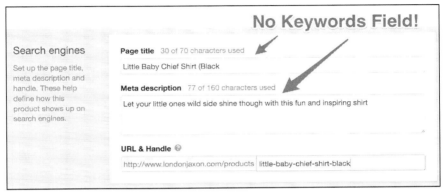

Figure 5-9

META KEYWORDS VS KEYWORDS

Right now many of you are thinking, *"Wait, I have heard that keywords are important, now I should ignore them?"*

This is a HUGE point of confusion. The keywords meta tag – a very specific portion of the page, no longer impacts SEO. Keywords and phrases within other areas of the page, in contrast, are **highly** important. Google and other search engines no longer consider the keywords meta tag, but they are smart enough to figure out what keywords and phrases have been used in the pages content, title and meta description. Disregard the keywords meta tag all together and focus on your titles, descriptions, and on page content.

Tuning your products

Because the keywords meta tag is of no value, it is critical that your on-page content needs to support the title and meta descriptions that you have written. Google is smart – if your title and description mentions "Transformer Toys", but the body content on your page does not contain that key phrase, Google may choose to ignore or under value the page. If there are too many page issues that display incongruent content and meta descriptions, Google can lower your entire site's ranking. Your pages content, title, and meta description should all work together harmoniously to tell the same story. The title grabs attention, the meta description is an attractive summary of the page, the pages body text should re-enforce the title and description. It is a simple yet profound way to keep your store on the path towards success.

Things to avoid

DO NOT USE STOCK PRODUCT DESCRIPTIONS

If you are selling a mass-market product like electronics, shoes, name brand clothing, or anything else that is not unique to your store, **do not** use the stock descriptions of the products. Google does not like duplicate content. The odds are that someone else is already using that exact same content on their site. If your site has the same content as another site that is already indexed, Google has no reason to add it to the search listings. Basically, if you do not take the time to create unique content for your site, do not expect to rank highly in search results. If you do not know what to write, or do not have the time, hire a content writer to do it for you.

NOT HAVING PRODUCT DESCRIPTIONS AT ALL

I am always shocked when I see a Shopify store that does not have descriptions for their products (Figure 5-10). Product descriptions may be optional in the Shopify admin, but they should never be optional for you. On-page content is **very** important. When writing, use the voice you have established for your store, common language for your industry, while including the keywords you want to rank for. Remember, do not focus on stuffing your content full of keyword and phrases. Try to sound as natural as possible while describing your product using 150 words or more.

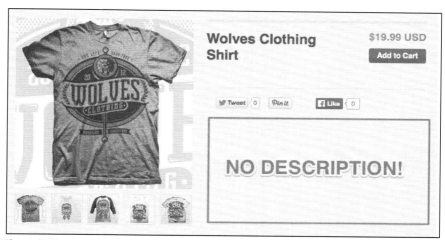

Figure 5-10

(Do not) Use Duplicate Content

Duplicate content is extremely harmful to SEO. Google and other search engines view duplicate content as *"spammy,"* and it can lead to your site being devalued in search results.

With Shopify, URLs are automatically generated for products and collections. If you have a product that exists in two collections, multiple URLs will be created for that product.

All three of the following URLs point to the same product:

http://merchbabies.com/collections/new-items/products/volumes-wolf-tank-top
http://merchbabies.com/collections/volumes/products/volumes-wolf-tank-top
http://merchbabies.com/products/volumes-wolf-tank-top

Because Google sees every URL as a unique item, two of these URLs will be treated as duplicate content and possibly count against your site in search rankings. To avoid this your theme needs to support *"canonical URLs."* A canonical URL tells search engines to always use the URL listed in the code instead of the URL for the current page. This means that you can have 100 URLs show the same product, but Google will only see and index the one canonical URL that is defined in your site's theme.

You can determine if your theme supports canonical URLs by looking at the *"theme.liquid"* file in your theme bundle, and locating the following code:

```
<link rel="canonical" href="{{ canonical_url }}" />
```

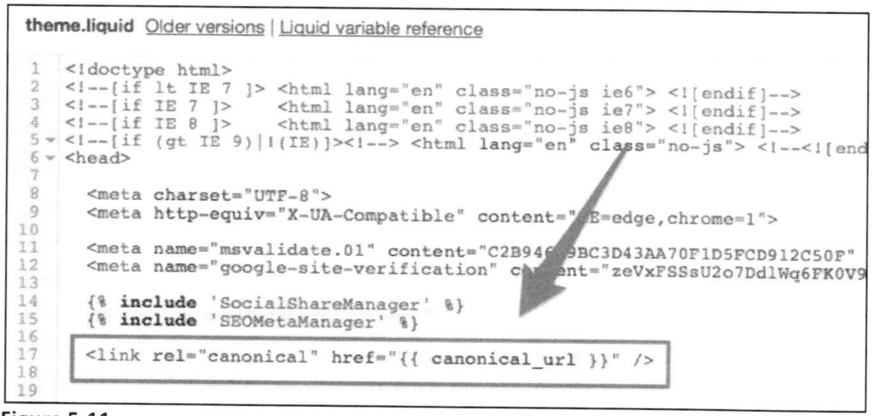

Figure 5-11

If you are unable to find it, you can always type it in yourself. Add it anywhere between the <head> and </head> tags. If you do not feel comfortable doing it yourself, reach out to your theme's designer or to a Shopify Expert.

6. IMAGE OPTIMIZATION

"You cannot bore people into buying your product; you can only interest them in buying it."

-- David Ogilvy

SEO For Your Product Images

Good product images play a critical role in SEO and customer conversions (sales). The goal of SEO is to attract users to your store. Once users get to your store, your product images are one of the first things they see. Having good images for your products increases user trust and increases sales.

PRODUCT IMAGES IN SEARCH

In 2010, Google announced that images searches passed 1 billion a day. That number is most likely much higher today. Aside from the Google specific image search, Google regularly includes images for products directly into text based search result pages.

If you have a great product image, it may be possible for your image to rank **above** the standard search result links (Figure 6-1). When a user clicks on the image, they will be given the option to go to that product page on your store.

Figure 6-1

PRODUCT IMAGES IN SOCIAL MEDIA SHARES

Kissmetrics.com, a leading online search analysis company, conducted a study on images in Facebook posts and concluded that posts with images vastly out perform posts with no images.

Interaction (image included)	Increase
Likes	53%
Comments	104%
Click Through	84%

Figure 6-2 (https://blog.kissmetrics.com/more-likes-on-facebook/)

The data clearly shows that images make an impact on user engagement. When an image is present, users are significantly more likely to interact with a post. When a user "*likes*" or shares your product on social media, your product image will be included. Having a compelling product image to go along with the social share will help encourage people to notice your product and visit your store.

WHAT MAKES A GOOD PRODUCT IMAGE?

Do not use stock photos – If you are reselling products like electronics, or clothing, do not use the stock photo from the distributor. Just like written content, Google values uniqueness in images used. Having images that are distinct to your store conveys a sense of authority to Google and to your customers. Unique images also allow you to be consistent with angles, sizes, backdrops and models. Consistency leads to a more professional look and feel, which in turn increases user trust and authority.

HIGH QUALITY IMAGES

Your product images should be clear, consistent and interesting. The best way to get results is by working with professionals. In the past I have used craigslist.com, local college photography programs, and the Shopify Experts program to find product photographers.

If you are on a tight budget or have a small number of products, you can take a DIY approach and shoot great photos yourself. Shopify has several blog posts on how to take product photos with little to no special equipment.

- http://www.shopify.com/blog/12206313-the-ultimate-diy-guide-to-beautiful-product-photography

- http://www.shopify.com/blog/15163633-how-to-capture-high-quality-product-photos-with-your-smartphone

WORK ON YOUR ALT DATA

ALT data was first introduced to the web when people had slow Internet connections and it took a long time for images on webpages to load. ALT data allowed page authors to describe the image that was loading.

Image *"ALT"* information also helps Google better understand what your image is about. If you are selling "Dodger Baseball Caps" you should update your product images ALT data to reflect this.

In the Shopify admin, simply click the *"ALT"* icon next to a product image and follow the prompt (Figure 6-3 and Figure 6-4). Do this for all of your product images and variants.

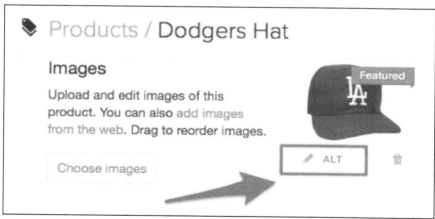

Figure 6-3

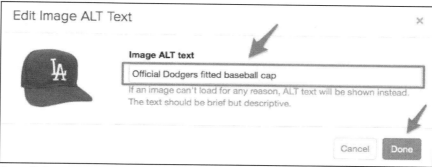

Figure 6-4

Another increase in SEO can come from how you name your image files. The file names can also act as SEO clues to Google. The example below outlines the concept.

Example:
- image0123.jpg
- official_dodger_fitted_baseball_cap.jpg

An image with a file name that contains the words "official", "dodger", "fitted baseball cap" is pretty specific. It is likely that the image is related to the phrases used in the filename. The more information you can provide the search engines about your products, the better.

I do not suggest going through your entire store and renaming all of your product images. You can use your time on more impactful SEO activities. As you add new products and images to your site, I would pick up the habit of adding key phrases into the image names. Every little bit helps.

7. BACKLINKS

"The objective is not to make your links appear natural; the objective is that your links are natural."

-- Matt Cutts, Head of Google's Webspam team

In the ever expanding and evolving landscape of the Internet, search engines like Google and Bing are gathering increasing amounts of data. To improve their search results, Google and others have started to look for *"off-site"* information about websites to help them determine search result positioning.

As the name implies, off-site data is data that is not gathered from your site. Even though the data is coming from sources that you may not control, you still have opportunities to optimize and influence. We are going to start digging into off-site optimization by talking about one of the most important and powerful aspects of off-site optimization - backlinks.

Backlinks

If you have not noticed by now, marketers and computer science people do not come up with clever names for things, we call it as we see it. Backlinks are, as the name implies, website links that refer back to your site and its pages. Sometimes they are also referred to as *"inbound links."*

WHY BACKLINKS MATTER SO MUCH

With so many sites and pages being added to the Internet each day it is difficult for search engines to discover new websites, and then separate the valuable content from the web spam. Producing high quality and relevant search results is critical for Google and Bing. Therefore it is important that they efficiently solve the problem of finding and ranking sites and content. As Google crawls the Internet it follows links on webpages and keeps track of how many times a page has been referenced.

Google interprets a link from site A to site B as a vote, by site A, for site B. It is basically a giant popularity contest. If you compare two sites with similar content and on-page SEO, the site with more backlinks and better off-site SEO will win in the rankings.

Search engine companies are smart, and have realized over time that it is very easy to get a massive amount of links pointing to your site. This is why comment spam happens, along with junk websites that are nothing but links. Unethical SEO marketers, use these tactics to try to increase backlinks and site ranks. Google combats this by assigning each site and link a score.

Google uses a system called *"PageRank"* or *"PR"* to determine the popularity of a site. Google places more weight on links from popular sites with more value. The PageRank scale ranges from zero to ten, ten being the highest rank possible. Having 50 small blogs link to your site will have a smaller impact on SEO than having a single link to your site on the front page of the New York Time (PR 9), or an article mentioning you in the Huffington post (PR 8).

Sites with a high level of trust and popularity will have a higher PR score. At the time of writing this, Shopify.com had a PR of 6. In terms of backlinks, having a site with a high PR score link to your site will help you gain search rank.

DETERMINING THE PAGERANK OF A SITE

The easiest way to calculate the PageRank of a site is to use a tool. There are many websites that allows you to enter a sites URL, and the calculated PR is shown to you. I have found that the easiest way to see PR scores is to install a PR extension into your web browser. These extensions automatically calculate the PR of the site you are visiting.

Below are some examples of PR extensions I have installed into Chrome and Firefox. I suggest trying to gather backlinks from PR 4+ sites in your niche when possible. Avoid links from PR 1 and 2 sites.

PageRank Display extension for Chrome
http://nemrod.se/chrome-extensions/pagerank-display/

Figure 7-1

PageRank 2.0 add-on for Firefox
https://addons.mozilla.org/en-US/firefox/addon/pagerank/

Figure 7-2

There are several types of backlinks, and each has their own unique weight to the search engines, and is displayed differently to users.

Contextual Links – These links have the highest SEO value and are the most desirable. They appear within text in an organic fashion and give Google context as to why that site is linking to you.

Example:

My brothers birthday is coming up and I had no idea what to get him. I was browsing the Internet last night and found a perfect gift, a beautiful hand stitched wallet *from Wallet World.*

The context contains information that Google can collect and use. The link itself contains the keywords "beautiful", "hand stitched", and "wallet." Reading further into the context we see that the wallet is a "perfect gift" for a male, and "brother."

URL Links – These backlinks simply reference your site. They do not have any context to the specific link, so they have a little less value than contextual links, however they are still wonderful to have.

Example:

My brothers birthday is coming up and I had no idea what to get him. I was browsing the Internet last night found a perfect gift, a beautiful hand stitched wallet from WalletWorld.com.

Image Links – These are links that come from images on a website. They are the hardest for Google to interpret and therefore hold the lowest backlink value. These types of links are usually accompanied with a contextual or URL link, especially when dealing with online stores. ALT tag data associated with an image can give some context to search engines.

HOW TO GET BACKLINKS

Like all things SEO related there are several ways to approach this problem. I like to classify backlink gathering efforts into three major categories – *The Good, The Bad* and *The In-Between. The Good* is what you want to follow, *The Bad* is what you want to avoid, and *The In-Between* are things that you can get away with, if done with caution and in the proper proportions.

THE GOOD

Link bait – Link bait is a fishing analogy. Imagine going fishing with terrible bait, something the fish has no interest in. You may get one or two nibbles, but you are not going to catch anything substantial or frequently. Like fishing bait, your content has to be good and market relevant. You should be generating content that makes people want to talk about it and link to it.

Take a look at Facebook, a majority of the content on your wall is likely people linking to articles and stories. If you have products to sell, you should know the market you are trying to reach. Write content that attracts your potential market share, and engages with them in such a way that encourages them to share it with others.

Shopify allows you to have a blog, so make sure to take advantage of it for SEO and sales purposes. Write content that encourages people to share it with others. Show that you understand the markets need. Write content that sets you apart from your competition.

Examples of link bait blog posts:

Why you started your business

How your products are made – quality and care

10 things that you are doing to improve your industry

How your products impact the others – success stories

3 ways that your business gives back

New product releases

Invite feedback from your customers

Interviews with your staff

Discounts on seasonal products

Closeout deals on products

The list of possible link bait posts is almost endless. Often the biggest challenge you will face is making time to sit down and write these posts. If writing is hard for you (I know it is hard for me), you may want to hire someone to help you write them.

Making blog posts regularly is also important. The schedule is up to you, but it should be consistent and the posts should not be more than two weeks apart. If possible pick a day, and commit to making a blog post on that day for 10 weeks. Hopefully making blog posts becomes a habit, and you can start to see the ranking benefits for your site.

Other sites you control – Do you have your own a personal website or blog? Write about your store there, post a link back to your store, and to key products you would like to rank for. Use a combination of context and URL links. Mix it up.

This also holds true for social networks. Update your LinkedIn account to contain a link to your store. Same with your Facebook, Twitter, Pinterest, YouTube and Instagram accounts.

Friends, Family, and Your Network - Expand your linking strategy beyond the sites you control by encouraging friends, family and others in your social networks to share your content. The goal in doing so is to raise awareness for your store, and encourage organic sharing and back linking.

Social Media – In the quest to produce the best search results, social media is a growing indicator of popular content for Google and other search engines. Social shares help search engines better understand your site's audience and importance. Be sure to include links in your social shares that point back to your store.

Contests – Contests are a good way to raise attention for your store and products without purchasing backlinks. Contact a blog owner and ask them to host a contest for you. You may want to offer the site owner some free products for helping you out. The point of holding a contest is two-fold, first as a marketing tool to raise awareness and traffic for your site, and second, to gain backlinks.

Brand Linking – If you have a well-established brand or product that you are selling, it may be worthwhile to find popular sites in your niche that mention your brand or your products, but do not have a link to your site. Sending an email to the site owner asking them to link to your site is a great way to grow market authority and earn backlinks. A quick Google search can help discover these opportunities.

Video Descriptions – If you create videos to show off your products, make sure to include a link to the highlighted product(s) or your stores main URL in the video description. Having a link in the description will help you build backlinks, and allow the viewers of your video quick access to the product they just watched. Users are much more likely to click a link in the video description, then to type in a URL you mention in the video, or do a search for your store.

Broken Link Building – If you come across a site that is pointing to one of your competitors pages, but that link is broken, you may have an opportunity to earn a backlink. Send a polite email to the site owner calling attention to the broken link, and suggest a working link to a similar page on your site. If the site owner is receptive, you just earned a backlink! Important: Broken link building should be very low on your list of link building practices. It is much easier to get people to link to fresh content on your site as opposed to finding dead links pointing to your competitors.

THE BAD

Often referred to as *"Black Hat SEO"*, bad SEO techniques consists of tactics that are known to damage your SEO rankings, and in some cases get you banned all together from Google search results. These *"Bad"* tactics are well known and monitored by Google, however many people attempt them regardless.

> **I do not endorse or condone the use of any Black Hat SEO.**
> **If you use them you will have reputational damage, and it is a**
> **highly unethical means of making short-term gains.**
> **NO NOT TRY ANY OF THESE METHODS**

Paying for links – In an attempt to build backlinks to their site, many people turn to services that sell backlinks. I did a Google search for "buy backlinks" and got 1,110,000 results. One site, http://buyhighqualitybacklinks.com, promises 8000 high quality backlinks for $129 USD (Figure 7-3).

Figure 7-3

Sounds too good to be true right? It is. Most services like this use their own web spiders to crawl the web and find websites with weak security and account creation processes. Once a weak site is found, they proceed to make spam posts that point to your site. These services basically pollute the web. If Google finds you buying links from services like this, they can severely downgrade your sites rank, or ban you all together. **DO NOT DO IT!**

Backlinks from Low quality sites – The number of backlinks matter to Google, but quality trumps quantity. I would rather have one link from cnn.com to my Shopify store than 100 links from blogspot.com accounts. Having a huge number of links from low quality sites is a telltale sign that you have used a link buying service. It is inevitable that someone with a new or low quality site will link to your store. That is okay. It is when all your links are from low quality sites that problems can occur.

Spam Comments – Similar to spam emails, spam posts contain little value, and often are comprised of links that take you to a product or service. As mentioned above, Google loathes this type of behavior, as do users of the sites that spam is posted on. To combat this many sites use a special attribute on links called "*no-follow*" that tells Google to not follow or trust any links posted in blog comments. Due to the use of the "*no-follow*" attribute on most blog comments, even if you are not caught making these posts, they have no impact on your SEO performance. Link buying services are known for making spam comments and posts in blogs and forums. Yet another reason not to buy backlinks.

Too many backlinks too fast – Real link building and growth is slow and organic, growing over time. Most sites that explode with thousands of backlinks in a small period of time have been mentioned by reputable publications online such as major news sites. If your site suddenly receives thousands of backlinks, but no site of high importance are linking to you, it is a clear indicator that something is amiss and Google may take action against your site.

The In-Between is a gray area where *The Good* and *The Bad* blend together into their own unique mix. These gray area tactics are a fine balance. Like walking a tight rope, when working with gray area strategy it is important to stay focused and balanced, making sure not to lean to closely towards *The Bad.*

Guest Blog Posts - Identify websites that cater to your niche. Try to find bloggers that write about your industry and have a strong influence. Attempt to find a blog that is updated frequently and has people commenting on the posts. If the blog is related to your industry or niche, you certainly have something to say. Contact the blog owner and ask if you could create some content for them. This content does not have to be about your products, but the article should contain a link to your store, even if it is only in a brief bio at the beginning of the article.

Discount codes - If you do not want to write content for someone else's blog, try to convince the blog owner to review your products. Send them a free sample of your products and ask them to write about their experience. To ensure a link back to your store, create a Shopify discount code for the blog owner to mention in the article for their readers. The discount code is a mutually beneficial strategy - the blog owner has something to give to their readers, the readers get a discount, and you get new customers, and links to your shop. It is a win-win-win-win situation. Using a unique discount code per blog will help you track which blog drives the most sales for you.

"Discounts? I Can't afford that!" – Yes you can! In fact, you cannot afford **not** to do this.

Lets be real here, and do the math on discounts. If you gave away a 10% discount code, and a popular blog writes about your products and links to your site. Because of that post you receive 20 orders, each with 10% off. You have then sold 20 products at 90% retail value each. Assuming that you sell your products for a profit, despite the discount, your will still be earning a profit on each sale.

Through this you have gained 20 new customers, and high quality links to your site that Google will love. If done well, this type of strategy will yield web traffic and sales for an extended period of time. Getting these new customers to write product reviews or share your site on social media will also help your SEO efforts.

Sponsorships - Ask a blog owner if you can sponsor their blog. *Sponsoring* is a way to purchase some advertising without buying a dedicated section of their site, like a banner ad. This can be a tricky one to pull off and potentially dangerous. It is technically *"illegal"* according to Google's terms of services, and can potentially lead to your site being penalized in search results. With that said, this is difficult for Google to verify.

Forums – Targeting niche communities is a highly impactful way to build trust, loyalty and backlinks for your store. Forums are typically focused on a specific segment. Becoming a member of a niche community gives you access to pool of potential clients. It is important to not be overly aggressive with posts about your products and store. Be helpful and only insert your links into conversations where it truly adds value. This is an *in-between* tactic because your posts could easily become spammy. You do not want to add too many links to your site too quickly, as Google will read that behavior as a spam tactic. Your ultimate goal should be to have other community members reference your products and services for you, as you become more trusted in your niche.

With all things SEO related, keeping tabs on what is happening to your site is critical. Backlinks are significant to Google and SEO, so you really should be keeping track of who is linking to you, how they are linking, and in what context.

One of the simplest ways to discover backlinks to your store is via a Google search. Go to http://Google.com and type in: Links:YourSite (where YourSite is your domain name).

Example:

Links:ShowStubs.com

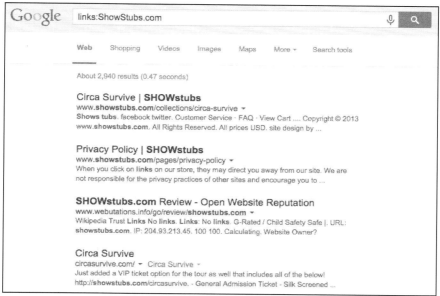

Figure 7-4

The results that this type of search produces are valuable, however incomplete (Figure 7-4). Google makes no promises of completeness or accuracy when searching for links to your site.

If you really want to dive into backlinks, using tools like https://SEOScanPro.com or https://monitorbacklinks.com will give you much more data, and will filter out any links from your own domain. The filtered data gives you a clearer picture of your backlink profile. These tools also allow you to monitor your site over time (Figure 7-5), allowing you to see when your store receives new backlinks, and the PageRank of the sites linking to you.

In the case of SEO Scan Pro, it will even warn you if a backlink looks spammy, so you can take action against it (Figure 7-6).

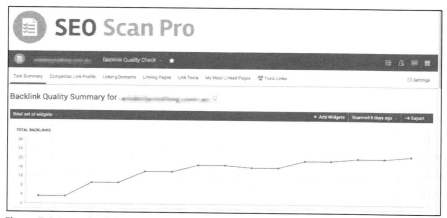

Figure 7-5 A graph of the number backlinks over time

Linking page URL (2)	Link text / Link type	Target page	Google PR	Home page Google PR		Status	
+ newleaflabs.com/portfolio-type/ seo-scan-pro/ SEO Scan Pro	NewLeaf Labs	http://SEOScanPro.com	/	unranked	▬▬▬ 4	OK	✿
+ apps.shopify.com/seo-scan-pro SEO Scan Pro — Ecommerce Plugins for Online Stores — Shopify App Store	seoscanpro.com	https://seoscanpro.com/	unranked	▬▬▬ 6	OK	✿

Figure 7-6 Detailed information on the site linking to your store

STRENGTHEN YOUR BACKLINKS

A great way to improve the strength of backlinks is to backlink your backlinks. Simply put, link to the articles and sites that are linking to you. If a site reviews your products, write a blog post about being reviewed on the site, and link to the article. Not only does Google measure links coming into a site, they also measure the links going out of a site – *outbound links*. A healthy site should be linking to other sites. This is your chance to both improve your backlinks and outbound links. This also creates fresh content on your site, something that Google also loves to see.

8. THE SOCIAL FACTORS

"It's because of this fundamental shift towards user-generated information that people will listen more to other people than to traditional sources."

-- Eric Schmidt, ex-CEO Google

Social Media Optimization (SMO) is different than Search Engine Optimization (SEO), but they are highly interrelated. SMO is an emerging field, and is gaining value in ecommerce. The tips in this chapter will improve your outbound marketing social media strategy, and increase your ecommerce sales.

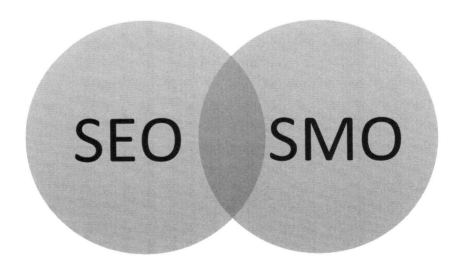

Social Gravity

When something is popular it tends to remain popular – it has gravity. Similar to how a YouTube video can go "viral," social gravity is gained through the repeated sharing of your product on social media. Pinterest's entire business model thrives off of social sharing and social gravity. Pinterest makes it easy to share or "re-pin" items. Without those concepts, Pinterest would not exist.

The following graphic outlines the lifecycle of content (Figure 8-1). The cycle starts with visitors discovering high quality content on your site. Then, your content is shared through social networks, at which time it is shared with others via Facebook shares, Twitter retweets, and Pinterests pins. The act of sharing functions as a SEO signal to Google. Google promotes your site in the search engine results, ending with more people discovering your content via search.

Figure 8-1

Getting Your Content Shared

Now that you understand the concept of social gravity, the question is, *How do I get my content to become popular on social networks?* The following measures will ensure that your content is ready to be spread to the masses.

AUTHORITY

When you write content, you have to be authoritative, and demonstrate to your reader that you are a leader on the subject at hand. When writing content for your blog and for your product descriptions, use a clear and direct voice. Make the information you are providing valuable and accurate.

It is also important to maintain the same identity across social platforms. Using the same profile image and logo in all of your social profiles, and in your Shopify store. This uniformity will help readers connect with your brand and quickly recognize you on each network. When writing content for your store or your social networks, maintain a similar tone and voice. This will also help to develop your brand, and your authority.

CONTENT QUALITY

People do not share low quality content. Make sure your message is clear, and that there are no spelling or grammatical errors. When creating content, ask yourself, *Why should someone share this with their friends?* If you are reselling products, ensure that you never use the stock descriptions that the manufacturer provides. Make sure that the content is consistent with the branding and image your store. The tone of a store selling high end men's shoes should be different than a store selling children's toys. Whenever possible, provide answers and solutions to your customers. Try to solve the question that they asked the search engine.

CONTENT PRESENTATION

Your content may be very good, but it will not be shared if it does not look good. Include images or infographics into your content whenever possible. Emphasize key points in the text. Keep it "short and sweet." Bite size content tends to be shared more frequently than long form content. If you are reselling products, never use the stock product image supplied from the manufacturer. Take some high quality photos of your products. If you are selling clothes, hire a model to wear them. People are visual, and high quality photos grab people's attention when scrolling through the steams of data on social networks.

LINKABILITY

After you have strong content and imagery on your pages, the next step is to make it easy to share across social networks. By now, we have all seen them - the Facebook, Twitter, and Pinterest buttons on a page (Figure 8-2). Clicking on those buttons shares the content onto the selected social network.

Figure 8-2

Your Shopify store should have social sharing buttons on every relevant page, especially your product pages. Your theme may not have them enabled by default, as each theme is different. Contact your theme's designer or a Shopify Expert if you need assistance enabling or adding them. There are also apps in the Shopify app store that add social share buttons to your theme. In my experience, if your theme does not come with social sharing buttons built in, you are most likely missing other features that a successful store should have.

META TAGS FOR SOCIAL MEDIA

In the same way that SEO Meta Tags give search engines information about your site, there are special meta tags that tell social networks about your site when your content is shared with them. Unlike search engines, there are several standards for these tags. The most popular standard, *"OpenGraph"*, is used by Facebook and Pinterest.

OPEN GRAPH TAGS

Open Graph Tags are relatively new to the web, and mostly relate to social networks, and not search engines. Google does not care about them, but Facebook and Pinterest **really** care about them. If you want to increase the visibility of your site on the web, you want to make social networks know more about your sites pages and products.

Open Graph tags help display information in Facebook posts when a user shares a link to one of your sites pages. This is very similar to the way that Google uses Meta Tags from your site in their search engine results pages.

Typically your Shopify theme should handle social meta tags for you. However, from my experience, most themes do a poor job, and offer you no control as to what image, title, or description populates when your content is shared.

To improve the ability to control social meta data, I developed "Social Share Manager" for Shopify - https://SocialShareManager.com

Social Share Manager is an app that automatically adjusts your theme and provides the needed social meta tags for all the top social networks. The app also allows you to control the title, description, and image that will be shown on Social Networks when your products are shared (Figure 8-3).

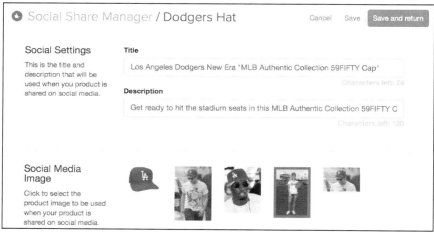

Figure 8-3

Engagement

To fully realize the SEO benefits of optimizing your site for social media, you need to engage with your customers.

Your business should have a Facebook Fan page, a Twitter

account, a Pinterest business account and a Google+ account. Each of these channels should be branded consistently with the same account image, and header graphic. It should be clear that all of these social channels belong to your business.

Once you have these accounts in place, you need to use them. If you have a product on sale, use the social media buttons on your product page to post it onto all of the different social channels. While you are there, follow the people that follow you. Start conversations with them – ask them how they like your products. Make suggestions for other products or services you offer. Above everything, be genuine.

I highly recommend reading "The Thank You Economy" by Gary Vanerchuk (http://thankyoueconomybook.com). It is an easy read that demonstrates how helping your customers will help your business thrive. Social media is an amazing platform for customer outreach and engagement. Do not miss the opportunity to convert customers into evangelists. Over deliver when ever possible.

A great tool to find social influencers is http://topsy.com. Topsy makes it easy to discover people that are talking about your business or the products that you sell.

Measure, Evaluate, Adjust

Like SEO, it is imperative to know what is effective, and what is not. Your customers may tend to group together on specific social networks. If you sell products for women or babies, odds are that Pinterest is going to be significant network for you, as Pinterest's user base is 80% women, with 90% of all posts being made by women.

We can make educated guesses as to what social network to focus our efforts on, but statistical analysis is always a good place to start. Luckily, Shopify tracks some of this information for you.

From your Shopify admin dashboard, find the *"Traffic Sources"* section and click *"View Stats"* (Figure 8-4).

Figure 8-4

Once inside the stats panel, it should be clear what social media platform is generating the most traffic for your store (Figure 8-5). *If this were your store, what would you do?* Pinterest has generated no inbound traffic, but 153 people visited the store based on links posted to Twitter. From this you can deduce that you need to spend more time getting your products onto Pinterest, and that you should be interacting with your clients mostly via Twitter.

Figure 8-5

Make Your Social Profiles Public

In today's world, having social media accounts associated with your business is necessary for success. Most social networks allow you to control privacy settings, including who can see your posts. This may be something you want to do for your personal accounts, but when it comes to business and SEO you need to remove all access barriers. All of your social media accounts should be public and viewable to the world. This allows people to discover and connect with you.

9. A DEEPER DIVE INTO SEO STRATEGIES

The tactics we covered earlier in the book make up the majority of SEO best practices, and are most heavily weighted in your SEO rank. You should focus on dialing those in before implementing some of the following, more technical, activities.

Code Tuning

Your Shopify store and all other websites are made up of code. When Google's web crawlers visit your site they look at the raw code that makes up the pages, not the visual version that your visitors see. The better organized your sites code is, the easier it is for search engines to interpret. Google currently does not punish websites with bad code, but it does reward sites with good code. SEO is a race to the top, so it is in your best interest to optimize your code.

CODE VALIDATION

Disclaimer: Google has openly said that code validation does not matter for their SEO rankings. Essentially, most of the code on the web is so bad that if Google only ranked sites with valid code, they would not have many sites in their search result pages.

"So Google does not penalize you if you have invalid HTML because there would be a huge number of webpages like that and some people know the rules and then decided to make things a little bit faster or to tweak things here there and so their pages don't validate and there are enough pages they don't validate that we said OK this would actually hurt search quality if we said only the pages that validate are allowed to

rank or rank those a little bit higher." – Matt Cutts, Head of Google Webspam

However, Matt and Google both encourage you to validate your sites code. A site made up of valid code is easier for search engines to work with and provides a consistent browsing experience across web browsers. Some SEO experts believe that code validation may become a ranking factor in the future.

One of the easiest ways to test your code is by going to http://validator.w3.org/ and entering your websites address (Figure 9-1).

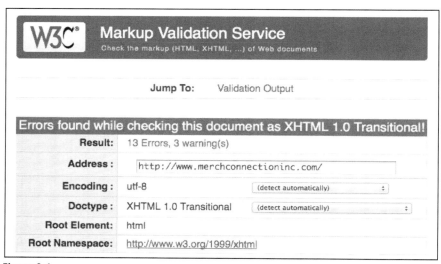

Figure 9-1

The validator will let you know how many errors you have. Please keep in mind that it is very rare for a site to have no errors.

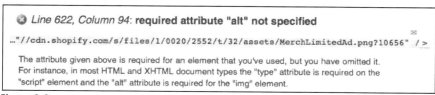

Figure 9-2

In this case, the validator is saying that there is a missing ALT tag on an image, which impacts SEO (Figure 9-2). The goal here is to catch on-page SEO issues, and to have as few errors on a page as possible. Some Shopify themes are better at this than others. You can always work with a Shopify theme designer to solve your issues, or you can hire a Shopify Expert.

PAGE SPEED

Even if valid code does not matter to Google (yet), valid code is typically faster, and page speed DOES matter for SEO and Google.

"A search result for a resource having a short load time relative to resources having longer load times can be promoted in a presentation order, and search results for the resources having longer load times can be demoted." – Matt Cutts, Head of Google Webspam

That is straight from Google's mouth – **SPEED MATTERS**!

Before you get too worried about your sites speed, know that by using Shopify you have an innate advantage over other ecommerce platforms. Shopify is highly efficient at delivering your content in a fast and stable way via the use of a CDN (Content Delivery Network). When I speed tune a non-shopify site, the first thing I typically do is move much of the content to a fast Content Delivery Network; a system that is designed to deliver content at optimal speed.

Even though Shopify uses a CDN, it can still be helpful to analyze your site and theme for other speed improvements. Shopify themes are beautiful and generally fast, however there are some factors that can slow your site down.

- The number of images being displayed on a single page
- The amount of JavaScript / CSS loading on a page
- Slow Shopify apps installed on your store
- Bad code due to Shopify app installs
- Theme modifications / settings gone wrong

A great tool to test your sites speed and get a report of any problems is Google PageSpeed Insights (Figure 9-3).

https://developers.google.com/speed/pagespeed/

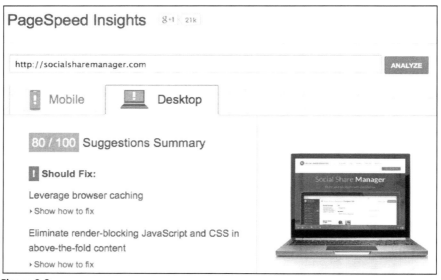

Figure 9-3

Google PageSpeed Insights is **free** to use and easy to run. Enter your stores URL into the tool and click *"Analyze."* If you are not a web developer, the results may be difficult to understand and take action on. I recommend that you contact your themes developer for help, or hire a Shopify Expert for the task.

Remember, site speed improvements should not be made solely for SEO. Site speed also improves the user experience.

Reducing Bounce Rates

Bounce Rate is the percentage of visitors to a website who navigate away from the site after viewing only one page.

When a visitor *"bounces"* from a page on your website, it means that they left your site after just viewing one page. We have all done it. We search for something on Google, and we click a result we realize is not the page we wanted, and within seconds hit the back button, and pick the next search result. We *bounced* back to the Google search result page, or back to the site that linked us.

A user can *bounce* from a website in several different ways. The most common form of a bounce is when a user presses the *"back"* button in their browser and leaves your site. Users can also bounce away by typing a new URL into their browser, or by clicking on a bookmark in their browser. A bounce can also come from the user closing the tab or window that your site is in. The least common form of a bounce is user inactivity. If a user has been inactive for more than 30 minutes, it is assumed that your website did not capture the users attention and they started doing something else.

Bounce Rate is also a measure of visit quality. High bounce rates indicate that the page is not relevant to what the visitor searched for. A 40% bounce rate is considered to be average by Google, however the average bounce rate differs depending on the industry and type of page. Users on mobile devices tend to bounce more than desktop users.

Why do bounce rates matter in SEO? Simple - bounce rates indicate how long a user stayed on a web page. If Google displays a search result, but most people leave that site within a few seconds it is probably not relevant to the user's search, or the users do not trust the site. If this happens often, it is safe to assume that the page will not remain in the top ranks of Google's result pages for very long. Google only wants the most relevant sites listed at the top.

You can use Google Analytics to check your bounce rates. Pay attention to the bounce rates from *"Organic Search"* or *"Google Searches"* (Figure 9-4). If you have a high bounce rate, it could be affecting your ability to rank higher in the search result pages.

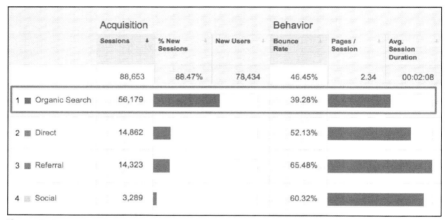

Figure 9-4

Tips on reducing bounce rates:

- Look professional
- Have good images on the page
- Clear navigation
- No advertisements
- No pop ups (including modal popups)
- Not password protected
- Price on product is clearly shown
- Site loads quickly
- Site is mobile enabled / responsive

Over all, give the user a better experience and your bounce rates will come down. Lower bounce rates means more preference from Google in search results.

Dealing With Out Of Stock Products

What should you do when a product is no longer in stock or has been discontinued?

Should you:
    A) Keep the product page up and tell users it is out of stock?
    B) Redirect users to a similar product instead?
    C) Show a 404 – not found error page?

This is a question that online storeowners have been asking for years, especially if one of their products has been ranking well in search results. Google has never given guidelines on this until recently. In March 2014, Matt Cutts, Google's voice on SEO and web spam responded to the following question in a YouTube video:

"How would Google recommend handling ecommerce products that are no longer available? (Does this change as the number of discontinued products outnumbers the number of active products?)"

Matt states that the size of your store matters, and suggests the following techniques that are broken down by store size:

SMALL ONLINE STORES

For a site with just a few pages and products, Matt Cutts advises against sending a user to a 404 – not found page. Instead, Matt suggests redirecting users to a similar product.

"It's sort of saying 'if you are interested in this cherry wood shelf, well maybe you'll be interested in this mahogany wood shelf that I have instead.'"

AVERAGE ONLINE STORES

An average sized online store consists of a few hundred to a few thousand pages (product pages, blog posts etc.). For sites of this size, Cutts suggests showing a 404-error page.

"Because those products have gone away. That product is not available anymore and you don't want to be known as the product site that whenever you visit, it's like 'oh yeah, you can't buy this anymore,' because users get just as angry getting an out of stock as they do with no results found when they think they are going to find reviews."

If a product is only temporarily out of stock, you should not remove or hide the page. If those pages are ranking in search results, you do not want to lose those rankings, especially when the product might only be out of stock for a short time.

"If it's going to come back in stock, then you can make clear that it's temporarily out of stock. If you really don't have that product anymore, it's kind of frustrating to just land on that page and see, 'yep, you can't get it here'."

If you need to remove a product, links pointing to that product will land on a *404 not found* page. The error page should have links to your collections, and have clear navigation to get to your homepage and other products.

LARGE ONLINE STORES

When Google talks about large online stores, they are referring to Amazon, Zappos, eBay, and sites like Craigslist. I have not come across a Shopify powered site that rivals a massive online player like Amazon, but there is no reason that you are not able to be the first!

Extremely large stores typically have a lot of product turn over. In some cases, products may not be available after a specific date passes. eBay is a good example of a site where pages have a limited life.

"We do have a meta-tag that you can use called 'unavailable_after', which basically says after such and such a date, this page is no longer relevant, so I'd like Google to not show it in the search results, so that's something where you can put a deadline on it, and you can say after this date, it's not useful to show therefore just let it sort of automatically expire on its own."

Example:

<META NAME="GOOGLEBOT" CONTENT="unavailable_after: 25-SEP-2014 12:00:00 PST">

I have yet to come across a Shopify site that needs to implement this technique. If you do, I suggest working with a Shopify Expert.

HOW TO REDIRECT PRODUCT PAGES

Shopify makes it easy to configure redirects. In the Shopify admin, click the *"Navigation"* link on the left side. Then click the *"URL Redirects"* button (Figure 9-5).

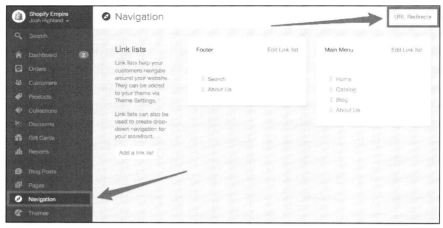

Figure 9-5

This will bring you to a screen that shows all your existing URL redirects. To add a new redirect, click the *"Add a URL redirect"* button in the top right corner of the page. A pop up dialog box will appear. In the box you can enter any URL pattern that you like for your site, and then specify the location that the user should be redirected to. Click *"Save URL redirect"* to create the redirect (Figure 9-6).

Add a URL redirect

Old Path

newleaflabs.myshopify.com /products/red-shirt

e.g. if the old URL was newleaflabs.myshopify.com/shirts, enter /shirts

Redirects to

/products/blue-shirt

e.g. /collections/shirts or http://www.example.com

Cancel   Save URL redirect

Figure 9-6

THE BOTTOM LINE ON MISSING PRODUCTS

When you discontinue a product it is best to redirect the user to a similar product, or to the products *collection* page. If the product is going to be out of stock for a short time, leave the page up and include a way for a user to be notified when the product is back in stock. There are a number of apps in the Shopify app store that provide this functionality.

10. SEO TOOLS

"Man is a tool-using animal. Nowhere do you find him without tools; without tools he is nothing, with tools he is all."

-- Thomas Carlyle

Tracking performance and site statistics is a key portion of SEO. By recording data, you are able to track trends and assess the effectiveness of your SEO efforts. There are a vast number of tools available to monitor and measure your site, but some tools are so powerful that they should not be ignored. The following chapter is going to focus on the powerhouse tools that are used widely in the Shopify SEO industry.

- Shopify Grader
- Shopify Reports
- Google Analytics
- Google Webmaster Tools
- Bing Webmaster Tools
- Google Alerts
- Shopify SEO Report Apps

Shopify Grader

https://ecommerce.shopify.com/grader

Shopify Grader is a free tool that is simultaneously simple and powerful. This tool allows you to analyze your store in terms of SEO, store usability, technical issues, and content management.

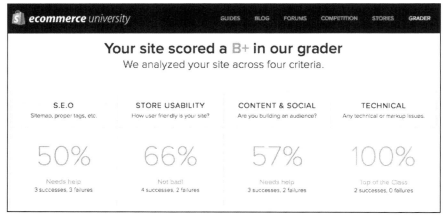

Figure 10-1

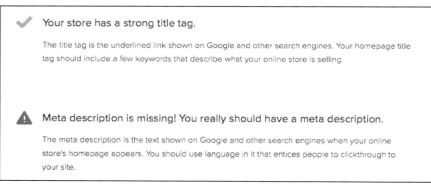

Figure 10-2

The results are fairly straightforward and give you some suggestions on how to improve the areas in which you are lacking (Figure 10-1 and 10-2). The reports are generated for a specific page. To maximize effectiveness, you should use this tool on every page and product. Considering that this tool is free, it is a good mechanism by which to run a simple analysis. If you receive a low "grade," you should use a more powerful tool to get a better understanding of what to repair. Hiring a Shopify Expert is also suggested.

Shopify Reports

Recently Shopify has rolled out a powerful tool for shop owners – Reports.

Your store's admin dashboard serves as a useful data tool by which to analyze your site's performance (Figure 10-3).

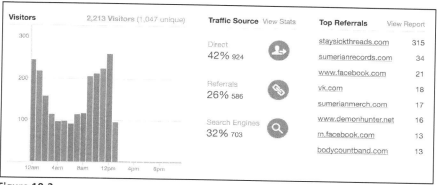

Figure 10-3

By clicking on the *"Traffic Source – View Stats"* link, you can dive deeply into the data that Shopify collects about your visitors (Figure 10-4). From the details page you can see what search engines and social networks are bringing you the most traffic. This is ready for use – no set up required!

Figure 10-4

Scrolling down on the Traffic Stats Page will give you some insights on what country your visitors are coming from, what search terms people are using to find your store, and the top referring sites to your store (Figure 10-5).

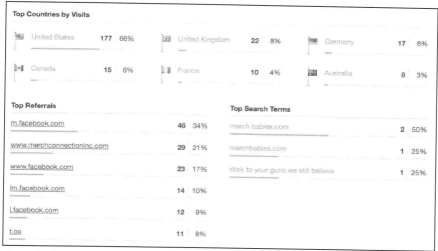

Figure 10-5

Clicking on the "Reports" tab on the left navigation bar will give you access to even more reports (Figure 10-6). *Note: Shopify Reports require a "Shopify Professional" plan or above.*

Figure 10-6

Shopify Reports are broken down into categories:

- **Products**: These reports show you sales based on your different products.

- **Orders**: These reports show you information based on your orders and related data including customer, region, and date of the order.

- **Payments**: Reports on payment transaction information.

- **Taxes**: Great for tax season – use the tax report to quickly gather the data you need to report to the government.

- **Traffic (beta):** View various breakdowns of your conversion traffic to understand more about where your customers are coming from.

All of the reports are powerful, but the Traffic Reports are particularly useful for SEO purposes. The Traffic Sources report gives you a breakdown of the sites linking to you, the number of visitors coming from those sites, the number of items added to user's carts, the number of times a user made it to the checkout page, and the number of times a purchase was completed. It even shows you the amount of money spent in relation to each site linking to you.

When I first started using Shopify in 2008, I would have paid a lot of money for these kinds of insights. Today, Shopify is giving them away! These reports are extremely powerful, and easy to access. Do not ignore them.

Google Analytics

http://www.google.com/analytics/

When it comes to tracking user action and traffic, there are few tools more powerful than Google Analytics. Over the years, Google Analytics has become the industry standard for measuring website audiences. Utilizing Google Analytics is requisite for the success of your online business.

Google Analytics offers analysis of: traffic sources, search terms people are using to find your site, page popularity, time potential customers spend on your site, and the geographic breakdown of your visitors (Figure 10-7).

The best part is that Google gives this application away for **free**.

Figure 10-7

How to add Google Analytics to your Shopify store

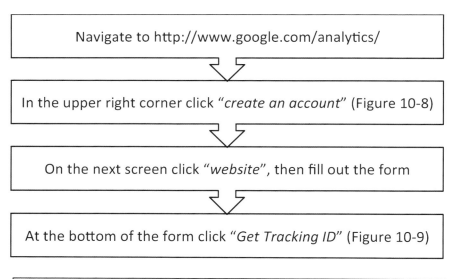

Navigate to http://www.google.com/analytics/

In the upper right corner click *"create an account"* (Figure 10-8)

On the next screen click *"website"*, then fill out the form

At the bottom of the form click *"Get Tracking ID"* (Figure 10-9)

Figure 10-8

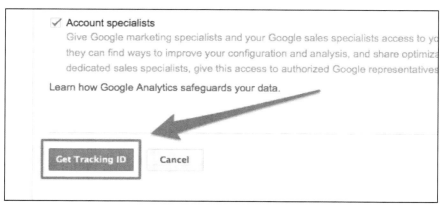

Figure 10-9

On the next page you will be presented with a lot of options. The only thing you need is the tracking code. The code starts with "*<script>*" and ends with "*</script>*" (Figure 10-10)

Highlight the tracking code and copy it

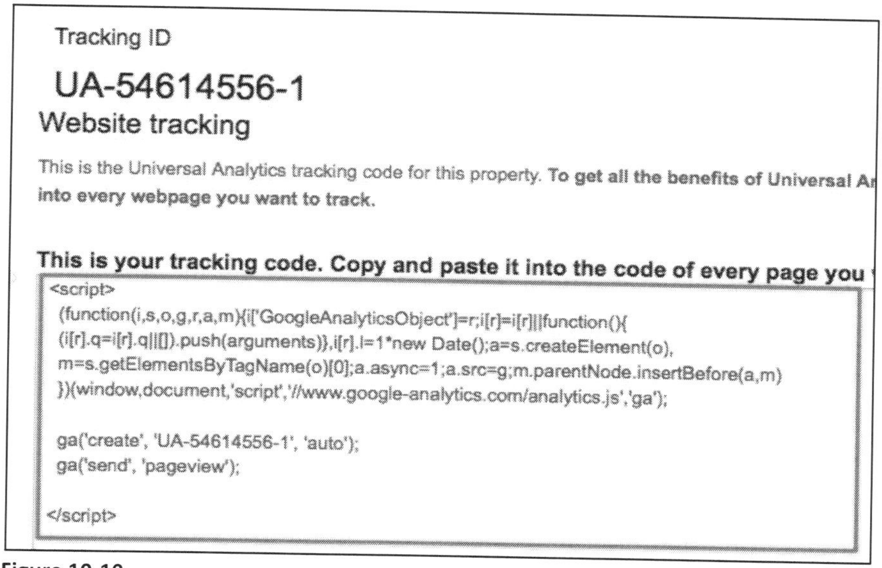

Tracking ID

UA-54614556-1
Website tracking

This is the Universal Analytics tracking code for this property. To get all the benefits of Universal A[...] into every webpage you want to track.

This is your tracking code. Copy and paste it into the code of every page you [...]

```
<script>
(function(i,s,o,g,r,a,m){i['GoogleAnalyticsObject']=r;i[r]=i[r]||function(){
(i[r].q=i[r].q||[]).push(arguments)},i[r].l=1*new Date();a=s.createElement(o),
m=s.getElementsByTagName(o)[0];a.async=1;a.src=g;m.parentNode.insertBefore(a,m)
})(window,document,'script','//www.google-analytics.com/analytics.js','ga');

ga('create', 'UA-54614556-1', 'auto');
ga('send', 'pageview');

</script>
```

Figure 10-10

In your Shopify stores admin panel, click *"Settings"* at the bottom of the left navigation, then click *"General"*

⬇

Scroll down to *"Google Analytics code"* (Figure 10-11)

⬇

Paste the Google Analytics Tracking code into the field (Figure 10-12)

⬇

Be sure to press the *"Save"* button in the upper right corner

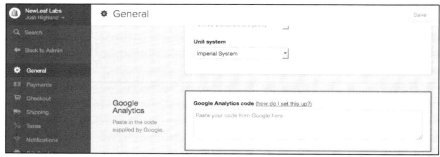

Figure 10-11

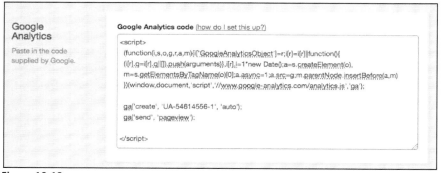

Figure 10-12

ENABLE ECOMMERCE TRACKING

Google Analytics also offers ecommerce tracking. Shopify automatically adds the appropriate code, but you must enable ecommerce tracking in Google Analytics.

In Google analytics, click *"Admin"* from the menu bar at the top

Use the drop-down menus to select the Account, Property, and View for your site

In the View column click *"Ecommerce Settings"* (Figure 10-13)

Toggle the switch to ON, click Next Step, then click the submit button (Figure 10-14 and Figure 10-15)

Figure 10-13

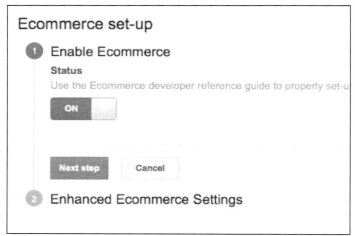

Figure 10-14

Figure 10-15

Google Webmaster Tools

http://www.google.com/webmasters/

Google Analytics gives you great information about traffic to your site, but Google has another helpful tool you need to use. Google's *"Webmaster Tools"* helps you understand how Google sees your site on the web. If Google needs to communicate something to you about your site, they use Google Webmaster Tools to send that notification. Anytime that Google gives you a suggestion about your site, you should listen to them.

Google Webmaster Tools:

- Sends you notifications from Google about site issues
- Identifies issues with your meta data
- Shows you search queries used to find your site
- Reports on the websites that link to yours - backlinks
- Tells you the number of your pages that Google has indexed for search
- Lists the keywords that Google has identified your site for
- Has the ability to removes old / bad URLs from Google's results
- Gives you statistics on what Google crawled on your site, and when it was crawled.
- Informs you of errors Google encountered when crawling your site
- Alerts you to security issues

This is not a short list, nor is it exhaustive. Moreover, this list will grow as Google expands Webmaster Tool's functionality.

Like Google Analytics, Google Webmaster tools are **free**.

Figure 10-16

How to add Google Webmaster Tools to your store

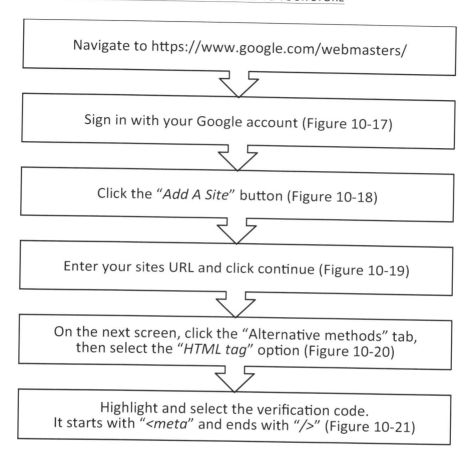

Navigate to https://www.google.com/webmasters/

Sign in with your Google account (Figure 10-17)

Click the *"Add A Site"* button (Figure 10-18)

Enter your sites URL and click continue (Figure 10-19)

On the next screen, click the "Alternative methods" tab, then select the *"HTML tag"* option (Figure 10-20)

Highlight and select the verification code. It starts with *"<meta"* and ends with *"/>"* (Figure 10-21)

Figure 10-17

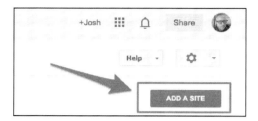

Figure 10-18

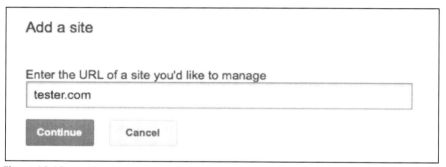

Figure 10-19

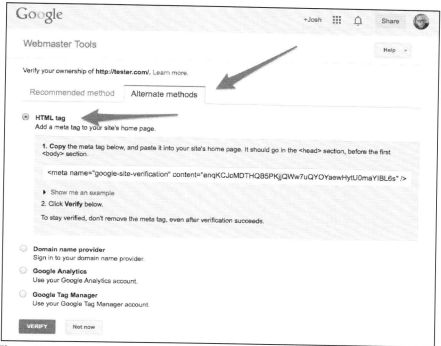

Figure 10-20

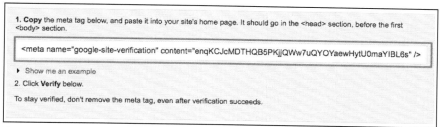

Figure 10-21

In a new web browser window or tab,
open your Shopify admin panel

Click *"Themes"* in the left navigation, then the "..." button on the top most theme. Select *"Edit HTML/CSS"* (Figure 10-22)

The Shopify theme editor will open

Click *"theme.liquid"* from the file menu on the left

Find *"<head>"* near the top of the code

Paste the Google Webmasters verification code on the line below *"<head>"*, then click the *"Save"* button (Figure 10-23)

Back in Google Webmaster tools, click the *"Verify"* button

You should get a confirmation that your site is now verified (Figure 10-24)

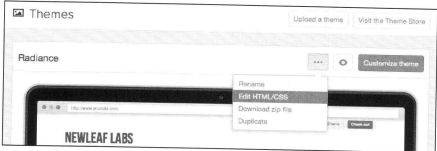

Figure 10-22

Figure 10-23

Figure 10-24

If your site fails to verify, make sure that it is not password protected. Google needs to be able to reach your store.

ADDING YOUR STORES SITEMAP TO GOOGLE WEBMASTER TOOLS

A sitemap is a file that contains links to every publically accessible page on a website. Sitemaps are helpful to search engines because they provide a way for search engines to find every page and product on your site. Website owners usually need to create and update sitemap files by hand, or use tools to generate them. However, because Shopify is such a great platform, they create and maintain a sitemap automatically for each store they host.

You stores sitemap is located at:

http://YourDomain/sitemap.xml

Google Webmaster Tools allows you to help Google learn about your site by adding a sitemap to their service. By adding a sitemap via Webmaster tools you notify Google about your site, and in most cases speed up the time it takes to be included in search results.

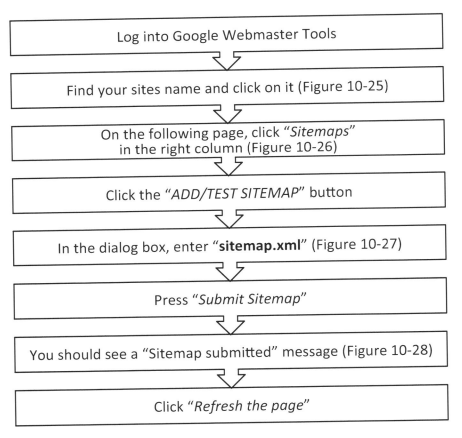

Log into Google Webmaster Tools

Find your sites name and click on it (Figure 10-25)

On the following page, click *"Sitemaps"* in the right column (Figure 10-26)

Click the *"ADD/TEST SITEMAP"* button

In the dialog box, enter **"sitemap.xml"** (Figure 10-27)

Press *"Submit Sitemap"*

You should see a "Sitemap submitted" message (Figure 10-28)

Click *"Refresh the page"*

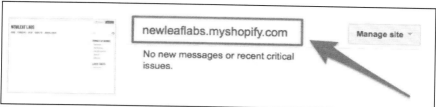

Figure 10-25

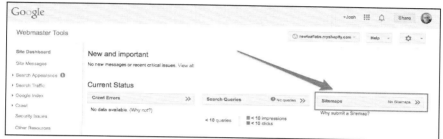

Figure 10-26

Figure 10-27

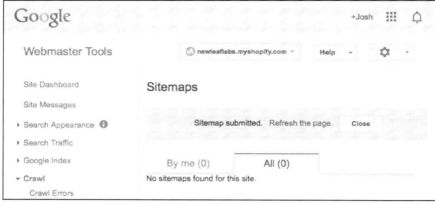

Figure 10-28

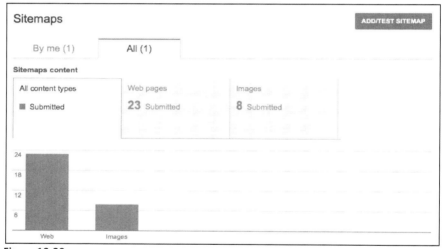

Figure 10-29

From this point out, Google will periodically check your sitemap for any new pages or products that you have added to your store. As long as you use Shopify there is no need to submit another sitemap to Google Webmaster Tools. Shopify will keep your sitemap updated, and Google will continue to read it.

Bing Webmaster Tools

http://www.bing.com/toolbox/webmaster/

Bing Webmaster tools are basically the same thing as Google Webmaster tools, but for the Bing search engine. Bing is a distant second to Google in the search engine race, but also offers helpful information about your site. Bing Webmaster tools are also **free** to use.

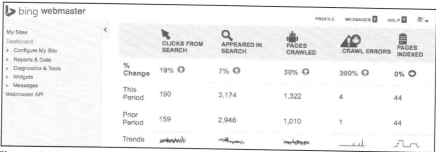

Figure 10-30

How to add Bing Webmaster Tools to your store

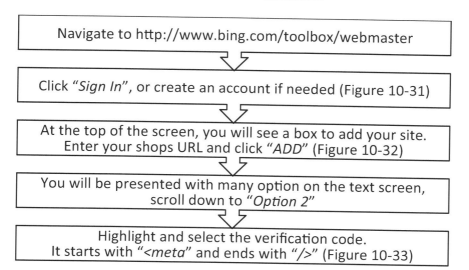

Navigate to http://www.bing.com/toolbox/webmaster

Click *"Sign In"*, or create an account if needed (Figure 10-31)

At the top of the screen, you will see a box to add your site. Enter your shops URL and click *"ADD"* (Figure 10-32)

You will be presented with many option on the text screen, scroll down to *"Option 2"*

Highlight and select the verification code. It starts with *"<meta"* and ends with *"/>"* (Figure 10-33)

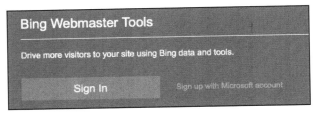

Figure 10-31

Figure 10-32

Figure 10-33

In a new window or tab, open your Shopify admin panel

Click *"Themes"* in the left navigation, then the *"..."* button on the top most theme. Select *"Edit HTML/CSS"* (Figure 10-34)

The Shopify theme editor will open.

Click *"theme.liquid"* from the file menu on the left.

Find *"<head>"* near the top of the code.

Paste the Bing Webmasters verification code on the line below *"<head>"*, then click the *"Save"* button (Figure 10-35)

Back in Bing Webmaster tools,
click the *"Verify"* button on the bottom of the page

If verification is successful,
you will be taken to a dashboard for your site

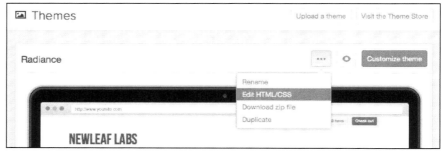

Figure 10-34

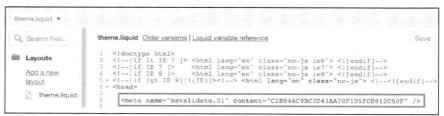

Figure 10-35

If your site fails to verify, make sure that it is not password protected. Bing needs to be able to reach your store.

ADDING YOUR STORES SITEMAP TO BING WEBMASTER TOOLS

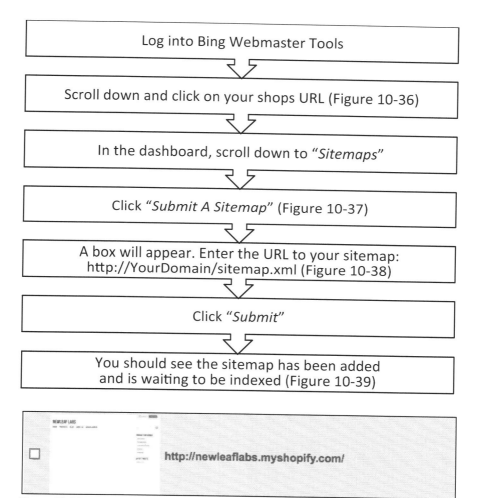

Log into Bing Webmaster Tools

Scroll down and click on your shops URL (Figure 10-36)

In the dashboard, scroll down to *"Sitemaps"*

Click *"Submit A Sitemap"* (Figure 10-37)

A box will appear. Enter the URL to your sitemap: http://YourDomain/sitemap.xml (Figure 10-38)

Click *"Submit"*

You should see the sitemap has been added and is waiting to be indexed (Figure 10-39)

Figure 10-36

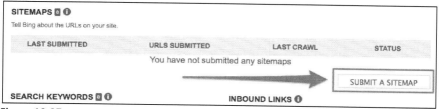

Figure 10-37

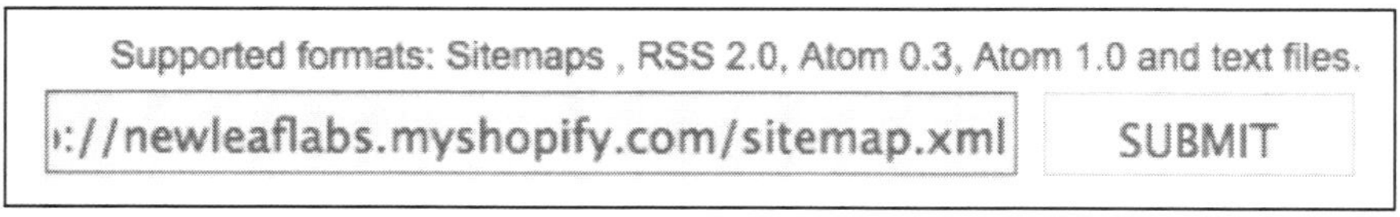

Supported formats: Sitemaps , RSS 2.0, Atom 0.3, Atom 1.0 and text files.

| r://newleaflabs.myshopify.com/sitemap.xml | SUBMIT |

Figure 10-38

SITEMAPS
Tell Bing about the URLs on your site.

	LAST SUBMITTED	URLS SUBMITTED	LAST CRAWL	STATUS
http://newleaflabs.myshopify.com/sitemap.xml	9/12/2014	Pending	Pending	Pending
			SUBMIT A SITEMAP	See all 1 with options

Figure 10-39

Like Google Webmaster tools, from this point on Bing will periodically check your sitemap and index new pages and products that you have added to your store. As long as you use Shopify there is no need to submit another sitemap for your store to Bing Webmaster Tools.

Google Alerts

https://www.google.com/alerts

I believe that Google Alerts is one of the most powerful tools that Google offers users. It is often underutilized as an SEO tool, but I have had great success with it and find it hugely valuable. Google Alerts is connected with Google's search index and monitors the web for words and phrases that you are interested in, and can even send you an email update every time it finds a new result.

Google Alerts has a huge range of uses, is extremely flexible, and is **free**.

How To Create Google Alerts

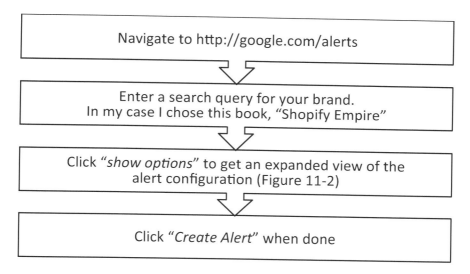

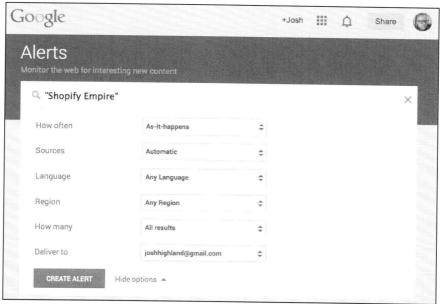

Figure 10-40

You can create as many alerts as you want. If they become overwhelming you can always adjust the frequency.

Set up these alerts:

- Your brand's name
- The URL to your store
- The names of your most popular products
- Your competitor's name
- Your competitor's URL

Setting up alerts based on your brand name and shop's URL will help you track sites that are mentioning you online. If someone mentions you in a favorable way but does not include a link to your store, contact the site owner and ask them to add a link. Knowing the websites where people are talking about your store also allows you to engage in the conversations.

By setting up alerts on your competition you can see what people are saying about them, and who is linking to them. You can use this information to help their customers become aware of your brand. When you discover a site linking to your competition, contact the site's owner and ask that your site be linked to as well. This will allow you to build a stronger backlink profile.

You can use Google Alerts to monitor any Google search query. It is only limited by your imagination. Go wild with it.

11. APPS FOR SEO

"There's an app for that."

-- Steve Jobs

SEO Report Apps for Shopify

Shopify's App store (http://apps.shopify.com) is a wonderful place to find SEO reporting apps that are tailored for Shopify. Each app offers a different service.

LEADING SHOPIFY SEO REPORT APPS:

- **SEO Scan Pro** – https://SEOScanPro.com and https://apps.shopify.com/seo-scan-pro

- **gShift SEO** - https://apps.shopify.com/gshift

- **Rabbit SEO** - https://apps.shopify.com/rabbit-seo

- **SEO Doctor** - https://apps.shopify.com/kudobuzz-seo

SEO Scan Pro is an app that I launched in early 2014. It is designed for Shopify storeowners that have the desire to seize control of their search engine and social media presence. Some of the features include:

- Weekly scans of your website for SEO issues
- Highlighting SEO issues, and providing suggestions for solutions.
- Tracking of your search rank progress in Google and Bing
- Monitoring of social conversations for references to your products

- Monitoring backlinks to your store
- Tracking of your competitions backlinks

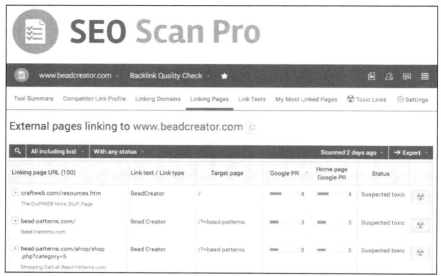

Figure 11-1

Product Reviews

As a general rule, whenever you get a chance to give search engines more information about your products, and to provide them with more quality content, you should take it. Product reviews are a great way to generate additional content for your product pages and to increase user trust. Reviews can also be a powerful piece of social evidence that proves that your store is trustworthy. Big ecommerce sites like Amazon.com and eBay.com are heavily dependent on customer reviews and feedback. Positive responses from customers help influence visitors into purchasing the product – the goal of ecommerce SEO.

User generated comments also offer the possibility of adding "*long-tale*" keywords to your site. These are keywords and phrases associated with a product that someone may search for, but your page is not specifically targeting. In the case of a messenger bag, a reviewer may leave comments about the strap, and the stitching, or how they use it as a laptop bag. These are words and phrases that you may not have targeted in your description or title, but Google could possible rank you for these additional phrases - increasing the possibility of you gaining visitors.

PRODUCT REVIEWS APP BY SHOPIFY

Shopify understands the impact and value that product reviews deliver. In 2012, Shopify launched their Product Review app into the app store - https://apps.shopify.com/product-reviews.

The app is free and does a great job of adding SEO friendly product reviews to your store. The review app delivers data in a format that Google can easily understand and index. In the search results page, Google will also start to display a 5 star rating system for your products, along with the current price and availability (Figure 11-2). These are items that encourage users to click into your site.

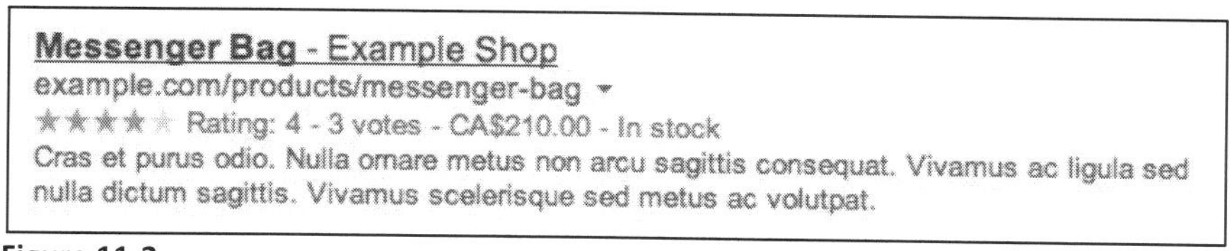

Messenger Bag - Example Shop
example.com/products/messenger-bag ▾
★★★★ ☆ Rating: 4 - 3 votes - CA$210.00 - In stock
Cras et purus odio. Nulla ornare metus non arcu sagittis consequat. Vivamus ac ligula sed nulla dictum sagittis. Vivamus scelerisque sed metus ac volutpat.

Figure 11-2

The app also makes a nice adjustment to your product pages and includes a simple star rating system with the comments (Figure 11-3).

Figure 11-3

HOW TO GET REVIEWS

Reviews can be challenging to get. They require users to take additional actions after they have purchased a product, received the product, and then had a chance to experience it. This life cycle can take anywhere from several days to several weeks.

Here are some quick tips on users reviews:

- Send a follow up email a few days after the product has been delivered. Politely ask them to leave a review.

- Offer an incentive for a review. For example, offer free shipping on their next order, or 10% off if they leave a review.

- Encourage your social media followers to rate and review your products to earn discount codes.

- For high-ticket items or custom made products, a follow

up phone call can be helpful to earn a review.

- If you are shipping goods, include a note inside of the package asking for a review.

- Do not purchase fake reviews, or write them yourself. This is unethical, and can possibly damage your search rankings.

- Make sure to take action in regards to bad reviews. Try to resolve any issues a customer has. Turn them into an advocate for your products.

Over all, getting reviews can be tough. Make sure that you do not become discouraged if the reviews do not immediately come cascading in. Each product market is different and it can take some time to find the tactic that best works for you, your customers, and the products you sell.

12. COMPETITION RESEARCH

"I looked at my competitors and I thought that, If they could do it, I could do it. And if, they are popular and doing well, I could compete with them."

-- *Tommy Hilfiger*

Competition is critical for free markets to exist, and the Internet is about as free and open as it gets. Unless you are selling something that is 100% unique and innovative, you will have competition online. Even if you do have a one-of-a-kind product, within weeks knock off replications of your product could be available for sale. If you want to make it to the top of the search engine results, and stay there, competition research needs to be a key component of your marketing and SEO strategy.

If you have a competitor that is outranking you in search results, it is in your best interest to investigate how and why they are ranking as such, and then take action. Let us look at some ways to research your competition.

Search Engine Result Page (SERP) Analysis

The first step in beating your competition is to understand who they are. A quick way to spot the competition is to identify the sites that routinely show up in the search results that you would like to rank for.

First, search for the keyword string that you want to rank for. Then, take note of the title and descriptions of the top ranking sites. Compare the structure of their titles and descriptions to what you are doing. Modify your activities accordingly.

On-Site Content Analysis

I will say is once again - **content is king**. Search engines thrive off of content, and utilize it to help determine the raking value of a site. When doing competitive research you need to evaluate how much content your competitors have, both on individual pages, and on their sites as a whole. As you research, ask yourself the following questions:

- What keywords are they focusing on in their headlines?
- How often are they creating new content?
- How much of that content is link bait?
- Are they using product reviews?

On-Site Tech Analysis

- How is their navigation structured?
- How clean / optimized is their code?
- How fast does their site load?

Backlink Analysis

- The total number of backlinks to their site
- Growth patterns in backlinks
- What pages have the most backlinks?
- What types of backlinks are being used the most?

Engagement Analysis

- What social networks are they most active on?
- What forums are they participating in?
- What associations / organizations are they part of?
- Do they sponsor any events / causes?
- What blogs are they guest posting on? How often?
- Do they host contests?

Competitive Analysis Tools

Developing a backlink profile on a competitor can be highly beneficial. A list of your competitor's backlinks will help you identify where to focus some of your link building efforts, and gives you an idea of what is working for them.

It is possible to examine the backlink profile of your competition by hand, relying on Google searches. However that is time consuming, error prone, and often inaccurate. Tools like SEOScanPro.com (figure 12-1) or monitorbacklinks.com can help you develop a good picture of your competitions backlink profile.

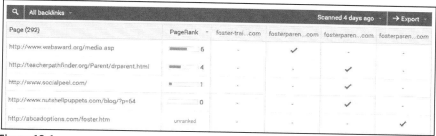

Figure 12-1

Helpful Competition Analysis Tools

- SEO Scan Pro – https://SEOScanPro.com
- SimilarWeb - http://www.similarweb.com
- SEMRush - http://www.semrush.com
- Open Site Explorer - http://moz.com/researchtools/ose

Once you have a good idea of the sites that link to your competition, you should approach those sites and attempt to get them to link to your site. I also advise setting up Google Alert monitors on your competition. **All is fair in love and online marketing.**

13. A DROP IN RANKINGS – WHAT TO DO

"Panic causes tunnel vision. Calm acceptance of danger allows us to more easily assess the situation and see the options."

-- Simon Sinek

A drop is search engine rankings can be devastating to a small business. First of all – remain calm and breathe! Next, dig deep and explore the possible reasons for the drop, then plan on how to return to being a high-ranking site.

Possible Reasons For A Dip In Search Rankings

There are a number of reasons why your store could have fallen in the search engine result pages (SERPs). Most of the time a dip can be explained by either an increase in competition, changes to your site, changes made to Google's search algorithm, or even a chance that your site is being penalized by Google for bad SEO behavior.

An Increase In Competition

Fact: You are not the only site that is fighting for the top position on Google.

Google SERPs are a high value land grab with power going to the "king of the hill." As you are trying to pass your competition, others are going to try and pass you. SEO work is not a one-time event. Think of SEO as a constant war, not a single battle, and your position needs to be defended. When you drop in ranks, someone else takes your place. All of the topics in the book are ammunition for you to beat them and reclaim your place at the top. Do not give up – learn what they are doing better than you, then use that knowledge to surpass them.

Major Changes To Your Site

The second most common drop in search results can be attributed to changes that have been made to a site – specifically theme and inventory changes. Your Shopify shop theme represents everything that is visual to the customers and search engines. Changing your theme can often change the way that data is delivered to search engines. If your previous theme was full of good meta tags for search engines and social, and your new theme does not present all of that data in the same way, there is a chance that search engines like Google will devalue your site.

Product changes also pose a significant risk to your SEO efforts. People sharing products on social networks and other sites typically link to products. It is possible for your site to have mediocre rankings, and have a handful of popular products that rank extremely well. If those products are no longer for sale, or you change the URL to the products, you may lose out on a lot of traffic.

To solve this problem, track your backlinks. Use tools like Google Webmaster Tools, Shopify Reports and SEO Scan Pro to track what pages on your site are popular and being linked to. If you need to remove a product, redirect the page to a similar product, or leave the page up and suggest related products. Do research before removing products and pages from your site.

Google Changed The Rules Again

Google and other search engines are constantly evolving. Frequently Google makes small updates to its search and ranking algorithms. Every few years Google makes a major update. The small tweaks do not usually impact most sites, but major updates have a rippling effect that impacts most of the web. These major updates tend to change how search and search rankings work.

Google's last major update, *Hummingbird*, makes searches more context sensitive and less keyword driven. If your site previously ranked for specific keywords, you will now have much more competition from similar keywords. An example of this would be the phrases *iPhone repair, broken iPhone, fix iPhone, iPhone replace glass*. Google has realized that all of these key phrases are basically the same, and that someone searching for one of these phrases is most likely interested in the others. In the past it was possible for different sites to rank for each of these key phrases. Hummingbird has changed that.

Google's Hummingbird update is just the latest in a series of updates. For a full list of Google algorithm changes over the years, check out http://moz.com/google-algorithm-change

There is little you can to do prevent being impacted by these algorithm changes, as Google does not give much advance notice. My advice is to maintain good SEO habits, and run ethical marketing campaigns. If you are not participating in improper SEO practices, the odds are that your store will be okay. If you are impacted, hire an SEO expert to help you correct any issues and get back on track.

Search Engine Penalties

Search engines like Google have the ability to penalize your site or throw it out of the listings all together. It is rare when it happens but it can be devastating.

Reasons for penalties:

- Spammy content
- Keyword stuffing
- Linking schemes to gain backlinks

- Low quality backlinks
- Too many backlinks too fast
- Broken links on your site
- Delivering different content to search engines and users
- Malware / viruses on your site
- Your site is slow

The dangers of *bad* SEO have been covered in previous sections of this book. The best way to not get penalized in the search results is to not participate in *bad* SEO behaviors in the first place. Focus on the <u>good</u> SEO practices that Google encourages.

If Google thinks you are involved in something penalty worthy, they will usually send you a notice via your Google Webmaster Tools account, and include solutions on how to fix the problem. If you need help resolving the issues or repairing your search engine standing, contact an SEO expert. Repairing damage can be costly, and very time consuming. Which should be reason enough to avoid unscrupulous SEO practices all together.

14. NO SHORTCUTS TO SUCCESS

"Success is the sum of small efforts, repeated day-in and day-out."

-- Robert Collier

By this point it should be clear that search engine optimization is not a one-time event, but rather a way of doing business, and a vital activity for the growth and success of your online store.

Patience truly is a virtue in the field of SEO. Optimization work is difficult, and sometimes takes weeks or months before the results are measurable. Do not get frustrated, and most importantly do not give up! By incorporating good SEO practices into the daily maintenance of your site, you are going to have an advantage over most of your competition. It may be a difficult race to the top position in Google, but never stop striving for it. There is no one-size-fits-all strategy to SEO.

Now that you are ready to dominate search engine results, sell more, and change your world - I would like to reiterate some key SEO tactics that every Shopify shop owner should start using today:

- Create quality content that is:
    - Readable – easy to understand
    - Usable – provides answers / insights
    - Sharable – something that others should know

- When writing content, always ask *"What is in it for the visitor?"* and *"Would this content sound out of place if my site was a printed publication?"* Put the visitor first, not the search engines

- Become an authority in your niche

- Become the source of knowledge

- Be a problem solver

- Focus on your site's organization

- Use great product images

- Participate in social networks

- Get other high quality sites to link to your store

- Never give up

TERM GLOSSARY

Adwords – Google's Pay Per Click contextual advertisement program.

Algorithm – A set of computer instructions used to arrive at a conclusion. Algorithms are to computers what recipes are to bakers. Search Engines use algorithms to determine what a page is about and how to rank it.

Analytics - A program which assists in gathering and analyzing data about website usage. Google Analytics is a feature rich, popular, free analytics program.

Authority - The amount of trust that a site is credited with for a particular search query. This credibility is derived from related incoming links from other trusted sites.

Backlinks - Also known as "inbound links" or "incoming links". Any link to a website by another website. Backlinks are a major factor in Google's PageRank algorithm.

Black Hat SEO - Unethical SEO tactics used to promote a site. Using Black Hat techniques may result in getting banned and unlisted by search engines.

Bot - See *Web Crawler*

Browser - Internet Explorer, Firefox, Chrome, and Safari are all examples of web browsers. They are programs used to view websites.

Canonical URL - A Statement within the head portion of an HTML page that contain the official URL of the page. This helps to avoid duplicate content issues within indexed pages.

Contextual links - These are backlinks that are embedded within the text of a piece of content, and are surrounded by other content. They are a powerful form of backlink, especially if the link appears on a sites homepage.

Domain name - The address of website. JoshHighland.com is a domain name, as is Shopify.com.

Duplicate Content - Content, which is very similar or identical to content found on another page. Sites with duplicate content will receive little if any authority from the search engines compared to content that is original.

Firefox - A popular web browser. A wide variety of plugins and tools are available for Firefox.

HTML - **H**ypertext **M**arkup **L**anguage. Web browsers read HTML code and deliver the results as web pages.

Inbound link - see *Backlink*

Indexed – When a web page's content to a search engines database for use in searches, the page is considered to be "indexed".

Keywords - The word or phrase that someone searches for when using a search engine.

Keyword density - The number of times a keyword appears in a piece of content, expressed as a percentage.

Keyword stuffing - The act of over using keywords during on-page SEO practices. Keyword stuffing can lead to penalties in search indexes and should be avoided. It is considered a "black hat" SEO tactic.

Link - An element on a web page that can be clicked on to cause the browser to navigate to another page or another part of the current page.

Link Bait - Content that is designed to encourage people to link to it.

Link Building - The act of cultivating backlinks.

Liquid Code - The computer language used by Shopify themes

Meta Tags - Statements within the head portion of an HTML page that contain information about the page. This information is often used by search engines to determine what a page is about.

Meta Description - The Meta Description gives search engines some context as to what a page is about. The description is usually displayed on search engines result pages, and is one the first impressions a user will get about your page.

Meta Keywords - A meta tag that contains a comma-separated list of words and phrases that helps to categorize the purpose of the page. Due to abuse in the past, the keyword meta tag holds little SEO value today.

Nofollow - A command found in either the HEAD section of a web page or within individual links, which instructs web crawlers to not follow the links on the page.

Off-Page SEO – Marketing work done on 3rd party websites that helps promote the target site. Backlinks are a good example of off-page SEO.

On-Page SEO - Work done to a specific page of a site to help promote its position in search engines results. Updating meta tags is an example of on-page SEO.

Open Graph Tags - Meta Tags that contain specific information that can be used by Social Networks like Facebook and Pinterest when a page is liked or shared.

Page Title - See Title Tag

PageRank - Google's proprietary link analysis algorithm that assigns a numeric weight to each document on the web. PageRank is one of many factors used to determine a page's placement in Google search result pages (SERP).

PPC - Pay Per Click. An advertising model showing Paid-for sponsored results alongside organic results. You pay when traffic is generated by your ads. Google Adwords is an example of PPC advertising.

SEM - Search Engine Marketing. SEM is often used to describe acts associated with researching, submitting and positioning a web site within search engines to achieve maximum exposure of your web site. SEM includes paid listings.

SEO - Search Engine Optimization. The process of improving a website's visibility in a search engines natural (organic), un-paid search results.

SERP - Search Engine Results Page. The SERP is the actual set of results returned by a search engine in response to a search query. A SERP consists of a list of links to web pages with associated text snippets. Search engine optimization (SEO) is aimed at influencing the SERP rank of a website.

Sitemap - A page or structured group of pages that link to every user accessible page on a website. Sitemaps help search engines find all of a sites pages.

SMO – Social Media Optimization. The process of improving social media presence to gain influence, and attention from search engines.

Social Media - Online tools that allow the sharing of information and creation of communities through networks of people. Twitter, Facebook, YouTube, Google+, and Pinterest are all examples of popular social media sites

Spider - See *web crawler*.

Theme - In the context of Shopify, themes are packages of templates that control the layout and design of your Shopify store. Themes are written in *Liquid code*.

Title Tag - A statement within the head portion of a HTML page that contains the title of the page. This information is often used by search engines to determine a page's content. The contents of the *Title tag* are typically shown in search engine result pages, and are often the first impression a user gets about your site.

TLD - Top Level Domain. This refers to the suffix of a domain name. .com, .net, .org are examples of General Top Level Domains. .cs, .uk, .au, are examples of country code based Top Level Domains.

Traffic - Users and web crawlers that are visiting and navigating a website.

URL - Uniform Resource Locator. Also know as web address of a web site.

Web Crawler - Also known as a *Bot* or *Spider*. A computer application used by search engine companies to traverse the Internet, gathering information about each web page it encounters. Search Engines like Google rely on web crawlers to discover and index web sites.

White Hat SEO - Ethical SEO tactics that are looked upon favorably by search engines.

18937333R00089

Made in the USA
San Bernardino, CA
04 February 2015